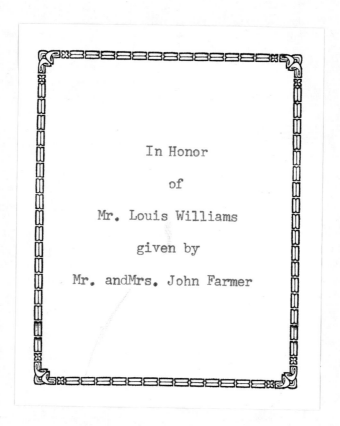

In Honor

of

Mr. Louis Williams

given by

Mr. andMrs. John Farmer

America's Coming Bankruptcy

America's Coming Bankruptcy

HOW THE GOVERNMENT IS WRECKING

YOUR DOLLAR

Harvey W. Peters

ARLINGTON HOUSE   *New Rochelle, N.Y.*

Library of Congress Catalog Card Number 72-91216

ISBN 0–87000–200–7

MANUFACTURED IN THE UNITED STATES OF AMERICA

Contents

Introduction
Why Blame Inflation?

The American dollar is in trouble. It is fast losing its value. In international banking circles the central banks of nations having strong currencies have shown every inclination to refuse to exchange their strong money for the weak American dollar.

The American public is being informed that the problems confronting the dollar have been caused by some "speculators" who seek to benefit by exchanging dollars for the stronger currencies of foreign nations. Absent, however, is much, if any, acknowledgment that if American money was in fact strong, then no speculators could render that money weak through the attempts to profit.

Officially, of course, many economic experts, including those in the Federal Government, have been tacitly admitting that the dollar is not strong. This admission is in the form of an acknowledgment that American "inflation" must be curbed. Unfortunately for the American public, even this admission concerning the weakness of the dollar has been couched in the same meaningless economic jargon and terminologies that have been employed for years in assuring Americans that their economy was strong and durable, and that continued prosperity was a certainty.

Yes, for something like forty long years the American economy has been described to the public in words that are of meaning only to those in the economic hierarchy. This has resulted in denying to Americans any opportunity to question, or to criticize, the actions of the economic planners. Obviously, this also meant that Americans, who were supposed to be the best informed people in the world, knew practically nothing about the state of their economy. It was equally obvious that this lack of economic understanding prevented Americans from doing anything but follow the economic course laid out by the planners and the Federal Government.

It should stand as the greatest tragedy of all time that Americans became like pawns to an economic elite. Unfortunately, those in positions of leadership did nothing to prevent this. Instead, the leaders in all walks of life convinced the American public that America is fabulously wealthy, and that all the public had to do was to spend. And the news media have cooperated in the national project of convincing Americans that they were the wealthiest people in the world. Completely missing was any reminder that wealth is ordinarily based upon work and production.

Whatever differences between factions have been brought to public attention concerned only questions that could be described as "dividing the spoils of prosperity," and these included arguments as to which faction, or which political party, had contributed the most to bring and to continue "good times" for America.

But now this public lack of understanding must come to an end. The American dollar is in trouble. Also approaching is the time when one can expect Americans to blame one another for the economic difficulties that can be anticipated to follow in the wake of the inevitable crash in the value of the dollar.

Up to now the whole problem of the dollar's declining value has been blamed upon something called "inflation." Once again, there is absent any explanation as to what brought about "inflation." Since the experts have been less than forthright up to now in explaining economic matters, it is appropriate for the public to develop an understanding as to the causes of the inflation that is wrecking the dollar.

Such is the purpose of this book. I shall start by stating that there is no mystery about inflation, and it need not be explained with fancy economic terminologies. The dictionary definition describes inflation as:

an increase in the volume of money and credit relative to available goods resulting in a substantial and continuing rise in the general price level.

This simply worded definition may seem to be inapplicable in describing the inflation that has been wrecking the value of the American dollar. How could the goods (and services) available for purchase have been in short supply (in their relationship to money and credit) in a nation whose citizens have been fully employed, and a nation where the national productivity (the Gross National Product) has been advertised as constantly increasing?

The answers to that question are supplied in the chapters of this book that follow. For the purpose of this Introduction, however, the suggestion is offered that not all forms of employment are associated with the production of goods and services that the consumer wants and needs. As a matter of fact, it shall be explained later that some types of employment cause the cost (and the prices) of consumer needs to increase, without contributing even slightly to the production of consumer goods and services.

To help the reader quickly grasp these explanations as to what has caused inflation, it is appropriate to supply an example of how a simple economy must operate. I do this because too many Americans have been led to believe that modern, "sophisticated" economic practices have eliminated those economic standards and rules established over centuries of civilized progress. Such a belief is wholly unsupported, and this I intend to prove.

I shall take as my example the hypothetical case of a simple agricultural settlement where most of the inhabitants till the soil, and barter what they produce with one another. Of course, some members of that community would undertake to be craftsmen, and to build homes, or to make clothing or shoes. However, this would pose no problem, because the products of the soil could be bartered for these, and by an exchange of products the members of the settlement could each assist in supporting one another. However, as this hypothetical community would expand and grow, there would be a need for teachers, for a clergyman, and possibly for some form of government administrator. The solution for supporting these nonproducers, who are, of course, necessary for the well-being of the settlement, is that each producer would contribute to the nonproducers a share of what he produces, whether these be products of the soil, or clothing, housing or shoes. But let us keep in mind one salient fact—*the more that some members of this settlement become engaged in nonproductive activity, the greater the output of the producers must be to support these nonproducers, or the producers must reduce their own consumption of what they produce.* Let us bear in mind, too, that the introduction of money into our hypothetical settlement in place of a bartering of goods and services would not change the conclusion expressed in italics by one iota. However, if money should be introduced to replace the bartering, one would find that prices of goods would increase, so as to act as a signal each time that it was necessary either to increase production or decrease consumption.

This hypothetical case explains quite simply what causes the development of skyrocketing prices that lurks behind the meaningless term "inflation." However, this case also should make clear that inflation is man-made, that is, it is caused by the actions of man and is not a product of nature. This means that some persons, or groups of persons, had to be responsible for causing American inflation.

Indeed, American inflation is not an accidental result of human errors, but was deliberately planned as an experiment by economic theorists. The grand plan of these theorists, in essence, was to assure a permanent prosperity by keeping purchasing power (demand) continuously above, or at least equal to, the available goods and services (the supply). In order to place their plan into effect, the theorists had to invade government; they were required to obtain control over a vast source of continuously flowing revenues; and, perhaps most important of all, the theorists had to brainwash both the public at large, and the opinion-molders of the public, into accepting what could best be described as a "goosestepping" by all Americans toward an economic millennium fashioned by these economic wizards.

The economic theorists had complete success in meeting all of these requirements, but circumstances played a part in attaining that success. First, the Great Depression brought the economic theorists into the top echelons of the Federal Government. Next, that same Depression was followed by World War II, and both of these emergencies justified a perversion of the Federal income tax so as to concentrate in the government the vast revenues obtained from taxing the earnings of all workers. Later, the theorists were additionally aided by the tax burden becoming hidden, as taxes were passed on to consumers as part of the price structure. Finally, an American public desirous of prosperity was easily brainwashed into "goosestepping" at the beck and call of the theorists. The opinion molders were not about to question an economic approach that was allegedly intended to raise everyone's standard of living, and specifically designed to prevent Americans from ever being poor.

In all of these developments, the economic theorists received the support of a highly mechanized news media (expanded by the addition of television) because the news media could not be expected to challenge an economic experiment that expanded national purchasing power, thus also expanding the revenues received from advertisers utilizing the news media, particularly in the retail trade area.

As with most theoretical concepts, the economic theorists' plan for permanent prosperity stressed an obvious fact, only to neglect the more practical considerations. The economic plan took for granted that the maintenance of purchasing power was needed for prosperity, and total emphasis was placed upon the spending of a continuous supply of money. Unfortunately, however, the theorists disregarded the practical fact that the wealth and prosperity of any nation depend upon a high-level outflow of physical goods and properties, including services needed by the consumers. Money was merely representative of wealth in the form of physical goods and properties. Hence, the overemphasis upon spending the money supply, and an almost complete disregard of the need for a productivity of goods and services to match the spending, could only result in inflation, i.e., the devaluation of money. As a matter of fact, the overemphasis upon spending and an ever-increasing money supply could only cause real wealth, physical goods and properties to dissipate, and such dissipation must eventually cause total collapse of the economy. This is to say that eventually the spending becomes far in excess of the assets

11

and properties that must be sacrificed to honor the money spent, something like the IOU's of a spendthrift eventually exceeding his wealth, i.e., his ability to repay.

Precisely such a collapse is suggested in the title to this book: *America's Coming Bankruptcy,* and the chapters that follow demonstrate how imminent this is.

America's Coming Bankruptcy

CHAPTER 1

Inflation Is Not a New Development

In the Introduction I mentioned that the present decline in the American dollar's purchasing power started in the year 1933. However, this was not intended to indicate that inflation, or the process of Americans experiencing a decline in the value of their dollar, originated in 1933. The fact is that the purchasing power of American money has consistently fluctuated both upward and downward with business cycles, that purchasing power being at its lowest level at the height of any American prosperity boom, only to be restored to a higher level during the depression that has followed each term of prosperity.

Nor is it any recent development to find that the blame for the drop in the value of the dollar goes unexplained except to mention the enigma known as inflation. The fact is that whenever the dollar has lost its value in the past, the condition has been blamed upon inflation.

Hence, before starting to explain the conditions that have caused the more recent (post-1933) decline in the dollar's value, it is appropriate to review some American experiences of the past with respect to the economic evil known as inflation. Among these, the "New Era" of the 1920s occupies an important place in economic history. It was this spell of inflation that collapsed into the Great Depression, which reached bottom in 1932. It is important to note that the collapse of the "New Era" provided the excuse for taking the actions that caused even greater dollar deterioration.

It is unfortunate that the American public thinks of the economy of the 1920s primarily in terms of stock speculation. The American public erroneously believes, too, that it was primarily the stock market crash that caused the Great Depression. This erroneous belief has directed public attention away from the fact that the 1920s were marked by a wild economic spree, participated in by practically all Americans, as the very phrase "Roaring Twenties" implies. This lack of understanding has prevented most Americans from noting the similarity between the boom of the 1920s and the boom of more recent vintage that has been causing the American dollar to lose its value.

A more accurate picture of the 1920s requires one to acknowledge that the entire American economy at that time had been inflated to balloonlike proportions. The economy was ready to collapse at any time that a sharp object (i.e., a serious depressant) would be inserted into the balloon. It was the stock market crash that was sufficiently depressing to prick the balloon, and the resulting deflation flattened the economy for the period known as the Great Depression. Such a description of the "New Era" is perhaps oversimplified, but it is nevertheless reasonably accurate.

That description is supported by remarks offered by the late Herbert C. Hoover, the man who bore the brunt of the blame for the economic excesses that led to the Great Depression. Hoover has provided us with his own interpretation of the boom of the 1920s in the form of a book entitled *The Great Depression.** In his writings, Hoover cited as a cause of the economic collapse the "deliberately created credit inflation" by the Federal Reserve Board that induced unwise investments and stimulated speculation on the stock exchanges. However, Hoover's recollections also include critical comment about the inflationary practices

*Included in *The Memoirs of Herbert Hoover,* a three-volume set published by The Macmillan Company, New York, in 1952.

in facets of American economic life other than the stock market.

In the process of Americans blaming Hoover for the depression, little attention has been paid to the fact that Hoover, while Secretary of Commerce, actually tried to warn the American public about the need for caution in pursuing what he considered to be unwise economic practices. For example, in a press statement issued on New Year's Day, 1926, Secretary of Commerce Hoover said:

> There are some phases of the situation which require caution . . . real estate and stock speculation and its possible extension into commodities with inevitable inflation; the overextension of installment buying; the extortion by foreign government-fostered monopolies dominating our raw material imports; the continued economic instability of certain foreign countries; the lag in recovery of certain major agricultural products; the instability of the coal industry; the uncertainties of some important labor relationships—all these are matters of concern . . .
>
> This fever of speculation is also widespread in real estate and, unless our financial policies are guided with courage and wisdom, this speculation may yet reflect into the commodity markets, thereby reversing the cautious buying policies of recent years. Psychology plays a large part in business movements, and overoptimism can only land us on the shores of overdepression. Not since 1920 have we required a better informed or more capable administration of credit facilities than now if we are to continue an uninterrupted high plane of prosperity. In any event there should be no abatement of caution in the placing of forward orders, particularly in view of the great increase in sales of a great variety of merchandise on the installment basis.

It should be noted that at that time, January 1, 1926, the Dow Jones Industrial Stock Average was about 158.00, a figure far removed from the high of 381.17 reached in 1929 (when Hoover was President), immediately before the stock market crashed.

Again, in Hoover's Annual Report as Secretary of Commerce, published in midyear of 1926, he said:

> No one doubts the extreme importance of credit and currency movement in the "business cycle." Disturbances from this quarter may at once interfere with the fundamental business of producing goods and distributing them. Many previous crises have arisen through the

credit machinery and through no fault of either the producer or consumer. . . .

That the Federal Reserve System should be so managed as to result in stimulation of speculation and overexpansion has received universal disapproval.

These publicly issued statements by the U.S. Secretary of Commerce were obviously intended to warn the public against unsound economic practices generally, even though they stressed the more obvious cause for complaint, this being the unwise speculation then prevalent.

However, as Hoover explained in his writings, these warnings had little effect because too many Americans believed that the economic system of the 1920s was completely insured against a financial crisis. This illusion, according to Hoover, was fed by highly optimistic expressions of American leaders, such as:

We shall have no more financial panics. . . . Panics are impossible. . . . Business men can now proceed in perfect confidence that they will no longer put their property in peril. . . . Now the business man may work out his destiny without living in terror of panic and hard times. . . . Panics in the future are unthinkable. . . . Never again can panic come to the American people.

These remarks seem strangely familiar when repeated more than forty years later in the atmosphere of more recent economic experiences. An even more direct similarity between the 1920s and the present involves the tendency of the Federal Reserve Board to inflate credit at any time that additional credit is considered necessary to correct a faltering economy. In 1927 the Federal Reserve had inflated credit (in spite of Hoover's warnings in the preceding year), and Hoover commented that:

One trouble with every inflationary creation of credit is that it acts like a delayed time bomb. There is an interval of indefinite and sometimes considerable length between the injection of the stimulant and the resulting speculation. Likewise, there is an interval of a similarly indefinite length of time between the injection of the remedial serum and the lowering of the speculative fever. Once the fever gets under way it generates its own toxics.

This renewed action to inflate credit was begun by the Reserve Banks in July by open market operations, and the discount rate was lowered in August. The fever of speculation began to get out of hand fourteen months later in the autumn of 1928. The vital relationship of this Federal Reserve expansion of credit to the stock-market orgy is easily shown.*

In his book, Hoover also criticized the banking practices of the late 1920s, thus clearly indicating that something more than the stock market crash had provided the cause for the economic collapse and the Great Depression. A few of those criticisms are worth repeating:

There were too many banks. In 1929 there were about 25,000 commercial banks, trust companies, and savings banks entrusted with the people's deposits. Of the commercial banks, 7,500 were national banks and 14,300 state. There simply were not enough capable bankers to go around among 25,000 banks. And there were some very evil ones in some large banks.

All commercial banks were permitted to loan excessive amounts of demand deposits on long-term mortgages and to invest in long-term bonds. When stress came, long-term assets could not be quickly liquidated, and depositors' demands had to be met by calling in the short-term business loans. That paralyzed business and employment. The supposed restriction on withdrawal of 'time' deposits and their use for long-term lending amounted to nothing, for if the banker refused to cash a time deposit before due date, his bank fell under suspicion.

But Hoover was not alone in his criticism of the economic practices of the 1920s. It is most appropriate to refer to the remarks offered by another famous American, simply because this other American celebrity did not have to defend an administration as Chief Executive of the United States. Here I refer to the late Bernard Baruch, a man who had unusual judgment in financial matters. Baruch's remarks, unlike those of Hoover, are much more general, and more biting, too. He expressed his views quite lucidly in a foreword to the

*The Great Depression.

1932 reissue of a book (originally published in 1841) entitled *Extraordinary Popular Delusions and the Madness of Crowds*, by Charles Mackay, in which Baruch commented:

> ... I have always thought that if, in the lamentable era of the "New Economics," culminating in 1929, even in the very presence of dizzily spiralling prices, we had all continuously repeated, "two and two still make four," much of the evil might have been averted. Similarly, even in the general moment of gloom in which this foreword is written, when many begin to wonder if declines will never halt, the appropriate abracadabra may be: "They always did."

It is interesting to note that in 1932 Baruch was suggesting that declines always do end, and it was in that very year that the decline of the Great Depression did in fact end by price levels hitting bottom, at least from the standpoint of stock prices. It is interesting to note, too, that Baruch, somewhat like Hoover, stressed the part that psychology plays in business movments. In the course of stressing psychology, Baruch literally scoffed at any attempts to measure this factor, whether by graphs, business charts, or economic thesis. He once again resorted to sharp language, saying:

> All economic movements, by their very nature, are motivated by crowd psychology. Graphs and business ratios are, of course, indispensable in our groping efforts to find dependable rules to guide us in our present world of alarms. Yet I never see a brilliant economic thesis expounding, as though they were geometrical theorems, the mathematics of price movements, that I do not recall Schiller's dictum: "Anyone, taken as an individual, is tolerably sensible and reasonable —as a member of a crowd, he at once becomes a blockhead," or Napoleon's maxim about military masses: "In war, the moral is to the physical as 3 to 1." Without due recognition of crowd-thinking (which often seems crowd-madness) our theories of economics leave much to be desired. It is a force wholly impalpable—perhaps little amenable to analysis and less to guidance—and yet, knowledge of it is necessary to right judgments on passing events.

One should not assume, however, that it requires the financial understanding of a Bernard Baruch to sense the weird aspects of human reactions to prosperity. As a matter of fact, even a seventeen-year-old lad displayed a sufficient wisdom to note the unrealistic developments that had accompanied an overdose of prosperity. This young man described the crash of a house-of-cards economic boom in the following words:

> Commerce and speculation here have been spreading of late like a card house, story after story and ramification after ramification till the building towered up to the sky and people rolled up their eyes in amazement, but at last one corner gave way and every card that dropped brought down a dozen with it, and sic transit gloria mundi! How people have grown rich of late! I often wondered when I heard how Messrs. A. B. C. and D. were worth a million apiece and how people were now worth half a million at least before they could be called more than paupers. I often wondered where all the money had come from and how such a quantity of wealth had found its way into the country. But here's the result of it. No matter!

These words are quoted here because the reference to the increase in millionaires seems to refer to a now-prevalent American economic development. Yet, these words were written on May 10, 1837, or more than 130 years ago. The quotation was taken from the *Diary of George Templeton Strong*, published by the Macmillan Company in 1952.

Even more appropriate than offering Strong's remarks in 1837 is to repeat what he said in his diary about inflation some years later, on November 28, 1865. On that day, Strong bemoaned the fact that his fixed income might be insufficient to support his family:

> ... That's very bad for me, a holder of mortgages and a receiver of a fixed income. I shall probably die a pauper. But inflation is a great fact for Trinity Church and Columbia College. They are leasing for long terms. ... My utmost hope is that I may be able to provide bread and butter, beef and mutton, for my wife and my babies.

This same complaint could be offered at the present time, more than 100 years later. Of course, the language could be modernized

21

by including a reference to "inflation hedges," the present day insurance against kiting expenses.

The inflation that diarist Strong complained about terminated with a financial crash in the year 1873. In that year (when Strong had attained age fifty-three), he made a diary entry somewhat repetitive of the words that he had first expressed as a young lad some thirty-six years earlier:

> September 20. To Wall Street. Nervous excitement seemed less, but bank officers and everybody said things were going from bad to worse, and the air was filled with prophesyings of woe. By twelve o'clock the Bank of the Commonwealth and the Union Trust Company had stopped, and the Stock Exchange had closed its doors. A wise measure, and would they might never be reopened. . . . The central focus of excitement was, of course, at the corner of Broad and Wall streets. People swarmed on the Treasury steps looking down on the seething mob that filled Broad Street. There was a secondary focus at Cedar and Nassau Streets where folks were staring at the closed doors of the Bank of Commonwealth and at the steady current of depositors flowing into the fourth National and then flowing out again with an expression of relief.

This chapter shall close with the reminder that any deterioration in the value of the American dollar is not a new experience. Neither is inflation a new development. Both of these have been continuously fluctuating with the business cycles. Perhaps these fluctuations have been more severe recently than in the past, but the explanation for this will be furnished in the chapters that follow.

CHAPTER 2

How the New Era Inflation Terminated (1929 – 1932)

The 1929 stock market crash tersely and decisively announced the end of the inflationary prosperity of the 1920s. However, this announcement was not immediately understood by Americans at the time that stock prices plunged downward in September, and again in October, of 1929. Even the economic experts refused to believe at that time that the "New Era" had ended.

Most of the persons that were associated with stock trading interpreted the stock market break as a type of "correction" of the precipitous climb in stock prices that had been terminated with the September-October price collapse. This "correction" theory seemed to be supported by some logic, since the Dow Jones Industrial Average of stock prices had practically doubled (from 191.33 to 381.17) in a period of just over eighteen months (between February 20, 1928, and September 3, 1929).

There were quite a number of persons, too, that held to the belief that the 1929 drop in stock prices had been carried too far. These persons reasoned that the stock-price break had brought share prices down to levels that were ignoring the so-called "intrinsic values" of quite a number of stock issues. To these persons, the low stock prices seemed to present just another opportunity for profit; that is they assumed that one could only gain by a purchase of shares at low prices, because the market ultimately had to resume its upward course.

Such a viewpoint was well expressed in an article appearing in the November 1, 1929, edition of *The Wall Street Journal*, which read:

The Sun is Shining Again

The Sun is shining again, and we will go on record as saying some good stocks are cheap. We say good stocks are cheap because John D. Rockefeller said it first. Only the foolish will combat John D.'s judgment.

Having had 70 years' experience in business, and having accumulated the greatest fortune of any individual in the world, the elder Rockefeller should have an opinion worth something, particularly when he backs what he says with millions of dollars.

But bear in mind that the statement from John D., Sr., published by Dow, Jones & Co. in advance of all other news services, said he was purchasing "sound common stocks." So if you do buy, know what you are buying.

Mr. Rockefeller says things are fundamentally sound. There has been no inflation in commodity prices, inventories or business in general. There was inflation in stocks and money. That has been removed, so that everything is now resting on a firm foundation, which means that industry can go on expanding.

No one can deny that thousands of people have lost money in the market through forced selling, but we repeat that every stock has an owner just as it had an owner when selling at peak.

But bear in mind that all security holders did not "actually" lose money although most of them were a little bent after the "debacle."

Ninety-five percent of the people of the United States still hold what they had, which, intrinsically, is worth just as much today as it was before the smash.

In the matter of yield it may be worth more before the end of the year as scores of corporations are expected to increase dividends. Others are planning split-ups and stock dividends.

Many small marginal traders who were worrying a few weeks ago over the heavy taxes they would have to pay as a result of profits on the long side are now worrying because they won't have any taxes to pay.

This opinion in *The Wall Street Journal* was typical of that held by many of the business and financial leaders for quite a number of months after the close of 1929. Many leaders reasoned that business seemed to remain prosperous in spite of the decline in stock prices, and this could only mean that stock prices had to move back up again.

Of course, with the benefit of hindsight, we know now that those who expected the American economy to move right along in spite of the stock market break were completely wrong. The basic error in the belief that the drop in stocks was temporary was the failure to associate the stock market with the balance of the American economy. Had this been done, it should have been readily acknowledged that not only the stock market, but the entire American economy, had been inflated to boom-bust proportions. A mere drop in stock prices alone could not correct this. As a matter of fact, the market crash had only confirmed the suspicion held by quite a number of Americans that the economic excesses (such as those mentioned by Hoover when he was Secretary of Commerce) must sooner or later come to an end.

Perhaps the greatest single effect of the stock-price break was the manner in which it disrupted the mob psychology of optimism. It was this optimism that had caused Americans to exercise blind faith in accepting ever greater quantities of a synthetic prosperity, and ever larger doses of inflation, as the economic boom had attained succeedingly higher levels. However, the stock market crash shook this faith to its very roots. The real effect of the crash was to cause many Americans to discard the wishful thinking fomented by mob psychology and to return to realism. And when Americans realistically appraised the state of their economy, they did not like what they saw. That this would, in due course, cause optimism to be replaced by pessimism should have been a foregone conclusion.

This change in public psychology would not permit the economic boom to be temporarily interrupted, only to resume its course after a slight pause. Instead, it was necessary to establish a basis for a new economic cycle, and to accomplish this it was required to restore public confidence at a realistic level. The first job to be performed was to restructure the entire economy to remove the excesses, i.e., the inflation, that overoptimism had engendered. If the American economy was to be restored to a sound condition, all factors of the economy, and not only the stock market, had to experience a severe deflation. Thereafter, it would take a period of time to rebuild a new prosperity. We know now that in terms of stock prices, this process of deflating the economy and restoring a new prosperity actually required twenty five long years. Stated in terms of the fluctuation in the Dow Jones Industrial Average, the 1929 high of that Average was not again duplicated until the fall of 1954.

The required next step of taking the "New Era" inflation out of the economy was a horrendous task. Practically all parts of the economy had to be deflated, or repriced, at new and more realistic levels. Obviously, the greater the inflation, the more the deflation that was required. And the inflation of the "New Era" had been great. This was so because, under the spell of a mob psychology of optimism, too many Americans had overspent, overinvested, overspeculated and overborrowed. The next order of business was to reverse these procedures completely.

In this reversal, the primary objectives were to exchange properties for cash and to remove debt. The accomplishment of these objectives had to result in the number of sellers of property exceeding the number of buyers. Again, this would completely reverse the condition just before the stock market break when the number of buyers completely outnumbered the sellers. This reversal had to force the prices of property to decline so as to reverse the kiting of prices that had marked the 1920s. And wages and salaries, too, had to be restored to levels suggested by the new prices.

The most logical item to sell to raise cash consisted of the shares of well-known American corporations, preferably those that were listed on a stock exchange. These shares could be sold on practically an instantaneous basis, contrary to the conditions pertaining to other properties, such as real estate, where months might be required in order to find a potential buyer. Of course, with literally millions of Americans eager to sell their shares, and with not too many potential buyers around, the prices of shares had to collapse. Although the prices for any other property also tumbled, it was nevertheless the

26

decline in stock prices that received the most attention. This furnishes the principal reason why too many Americans developed the belief that the Great Depression was caused primarily by the stock market crash.

Occasionally, between the years 1929 and 1932, stock prices would halt their downward plunge and a sharp "snap-up," or "recovery," would take place. These "recoveries" generally occurred every time that the then President, Herbert Hoover, would announce some new Federal Government procedure that was intended to interrupt the economic holocaust. But the Wall Street stock fraternity, having learned its lesson, was no longer inclined to indulge in the luxury of optimism, and the Wall Streeters applied to Hoover's well-intended efforts the undignified interpretation that he was "pulling white rabbits out of a hat." The one-time disciples of the "New Era" philosophy had become quite thoroughly chastened. These one-time optimists adopted a doubting-Thomas attitude concerning even sincere efforts to restore a factor of economic stability.

As a matter of fact, the degree of care that had been exercised in purchasing shares meant very little during the precipitous and long-continued drop in stock prices that started in late 1929, because all holders of stocks found that the values of their holdings plummeted to almost nothing. It mattered not what skill or reasoning had been employed in choosing stocks. They all took a beating. It could be concluded, however, that the skill or reasoning used in the purchase of shares later played a part in deciding how fast the stock buyer would "take his lumps" when prices broke.

For example, those who bought high fliers found that these could fly down, too. These were most often the cheaper quality stocks (acknowledged to be "cats and dogs" after the crash), and their value dropped so fast after the decline started that the certificates were soon referred to as "wallpaper." As a matter of fact, the certificates were in some cases used as wallpaper to decorate the club rooms of their disillusioned holders.

On the other hand, those who had bought good quality stocks found, too, that their holdings were not immune to the drop in values. When cash became in ever greater demand as the drop in

27

prices continued, it was only the quality shares that retained a sufficient market value to make a sale of such shares worth the effort from the standpoint of producing cash upon sale. At that point of time, the quality shares that had been put away in lock boxes to be forgotten were remembered. However, the price that these shares brought upon sale was often a small fraction of the original cost to the shareholders.

Hence, by July of 1932 the continuous decline in share values brought even the shares of well-known corporations down to figures that resembled bargain-basement prices when compared with their 1929 highs. The following table clearly demonstrates this:

TABLE 1

	Common Stock Share Prices	
	1929 High	1932 Low
Allied Chemical Corporation	354–3/4	42–1/2
American Motors Corporation	118–7/8	7–7/8
Beatrice Foods Company	92	7
Bendix Corporation	104–3/8	4–1/2
Chrysler Corporation	135	5
Du Pont (E.I.) de Nemours & Co.	231	22
General Foods Corp.	81–3/4	19–5/8
General Motors Corp.	91–3/4	7–1/2
Interstate Department Stores, Inc.	93–1/2	1–1/2
Minnesota Mining and Manufacturing	14–1/2	4–1/2
Montgomery Ward & Co. Inc.	156–7/8	3–1/2
Radio Corporation of America	114–3/4	2–1/2
Republic Steel Corporation	95–3/4	1–7/8
Standard Oil of California	81–7/8	15–1/8
Standard Oil of New Jersey	83	19–7/8
Union Carbide Co.	140	15–1/2
United Fruit Co.	158–1/2	10–1/4
United States Steel Corp.	261–3/4	21–1/4

As these prices of some well-known stocks should suggest, by July of 1932 the stock market was so deflated that the sale of the shares of almost any corporation could no longer produce any appreciable quantity of cash. Perhaps this condition more than anything else granted the market value of shares a reprieve from any further bombardment. In many instances, the decline had carried share prices to just above zero—the absolute minimum. And, at this particular point, the stock market decline that had started in the fall of 1929 began to bottom out.

It was then (July 1932) that the Dow Jones Industrial Stock Average reached the low point of 41.22. And thereafter occurred a recovery, or snap back, in stock prices, but this recovery encountered difficulty in moving upward at the time of the "bank holiday" (February 1933). However, during the last stage of the economic upheaval that had begun in late 1929 the Dow Jones Industrial Average held at 50.16, or somewhat above the 41.22 low point of July 1932. This Dow Jones Industrial Average low of 41.22 was barely more than one-tenth of the high of 381.17 attained before the 1929 break had started. And when the July 1932 low of 41.22 was not thereafter violated, this indicated, at least from the standpoint of stock prices, that the deflation in share market values had run its course.

There was a considerable significance to be attached to the fact that stock prices had hit bottom. Those with experience in the relationship between stock prices and business affairs knew as early as July 1932 that the stock market was forecasting that the absolute bottom of the Great Depression had been reached. And July 1932 was some four months before Franklin D. Roosevelt was elected President of the United States to succeed Herbert Hoover, and even more months before President Roosevelt took office. Hence, in the cold judgment of the market place, the Great Depression had hit bottom no matter which man was to be elected Chief Executive in November 1932, and irrespective of the political party that would receive the voters' command to guide American political affairs after the November elections. One could, of course, include the comment that by July 1932 the deflation of the economy had been so complete that there remained little left to deflate.

As is the case with the end of any holocaust, the July 1932 termination of the stock-price plunge announced, however half-heartedly, that "The Sun is Shining Again," even as *The Wall Street Journal* article had somewhat prematurely suggested on November 1, 1929, almost three years earlier. Of course, in July 1932, the sun could only shine upon a bleak and desolate economic terrain from which the

29

storm had swept away jobs, savings and fortunes. Nevertheless, the after-the-storm mopping-up operations had to begin, because the termination of the stock-price decline now provided a new basis for establishing values at all levels of economic activity. And this terminated three years of uncertainty as to where the bottom would be.

The establishment of a new stock-price level prompted the start of the somber task of effecting a vast number of corporate reorganizations, foreclosures, bankruptcies and bank liquidations. The lower level of values offered at least the suggestion as to who owned what, i.e., the creditors or the debtors, these often being the bondholders or the stockholders. This question being resolved in each individual case, there followed the transfer of the ownership, the title and the management of practically all types of properties from the debtors and the former equity holders to the creditors and the bondholders who could legally claim these properties as the new owners under the new set of lower values.

However, the most serious problem concerned the matter of finding jobs for those without work and without means for support. The opportunities for employment had collapsed about as quickly as investment and property values had dropped and savings and fortunes had evaporated. This the grim labor statistics revealed:

TABLE 2

Civilian Labor Force—
Employed and Unemployed

	Total Employed Civilian Labor Force	Number of Unemployed
	(millions of persons)	
1929	47.63	1.55
1930	45.48	4.34
1931	42.40	8.02
1932	38.94	12.06

Source: Bureau of Labor Statistics.

Unemployment had always been associated with financial panics in the history of the American economy. However, the tangled mess of economic affairs in the early 1930s involved some entirely new

30

problems because of the growth of large-scale corporate empires that had been a by-product of the considerable expansion in mass production during the 1920s. Mass production had required for the most part only unskilled factory hands, and hence the millions of unemployed had no skill or craft with which to make a living. And millions of investors were in the same plight as the unemployed workers, because these investors owned fragments of the huge mass-production corporations, whether stocks or some other form of security. These investors faced the depression with little or no understanding about industry, business or finance, even though the theorists had euphemistically dubbed them "capitalists" during the 1920s. Moreover the mass-production complexes had required the services of thousands of clerical employees who, like the factory hands, were trained in nothing more than to perform routine administrative tasks.*

The exploitation of the benefits of mass production had been wonderful while it lasted. Mass production had permitted the employment of those with minimum skills. It had made jobs easy to get for those who did not want to struggle or develop a trade, skill or craft. It furnished employment opportunities for those who had no work experience. These apparent benefits were as applicable to those who had wanted office employment as for those who sought work in the factories. All this had contributed toward making the investment of funds easy. Stocks and bonds could be purchased over the counter through almost any bank or real estate office, and sometimes through attorneys, too.

However, when the depression broke, pandemonium was let loose. Those who had lost their jobs often had no skill or experience to fall back upon. Their only hope was some day to regain the job they had lost. And those who had been performing simple office tasks proved to be the most expendable from a job standpoint. Somewhat ironically, those who had enjoyed higher amounts of compensation,

*These clerical employees had been derisively dubbed "pencil pushers" in the early 1900s by those who had a skill or a craft. But this term was dropped, perhaps because of the high pay they later commanded, and also perhaps because college graduates eventually swelled the ranks of the former "pencil pushers."

and the fanciest job titles, were the first to lose their jobs. This happened because under depressed conditions everyone's economic worth had to be reappraised in a coldly realistic manner. And the new standard was—what did the employee contribute to true production, and at what cost to the employer?

The application of these new depression standards hit hardest those who had benefited the most during the now vanished "New Era," and those that had theretofore expended the least effort. For example, the college graduates who had taken the easy road to riches by selling investments, real estate and life insurance, found themselves during the depression with no customers. The worldly-wise who had shunned degrading employment for the more dignified course of operating their own business soon learned that operating a business during a depression furnished no means of support. Those who had discontinued work because they had amassed a fortune during the boom often found they no longer had a fortune, and they had forgotten how to work. Perhaps the most weird of the depression developments concerned a group known as "efficiency experts." This job calling had developed in the late 1920s for the important purpose of expediting production. But when this work function was reappraised in the cold realism of the depression, the conclusion was that "efficiency experts" really served no valid purpose. And the sarcastic comment was oft repeated—"When the crash came, the efficiency experts were the first to be let out."*

The new variety of problems that confronted the American people in the early 1930s was not restricted to the predicaments confronting those who lost jobs or investments. The problems also confronted the American consumers. The consumer, you see, had been engaged in some different purchasing procedures during the prosperous 1920s. For one thing, the list of so-called necessities of life had been greatly expanded to include automobiles, radios, electrical household equipment, and many other high-cost items. This had increased the size

---

*Actually there was nothing new or different about these developments. So long as success continues, everyone is assumed to be contributing to the success. But when the success comes to an end, then the worth of everyone is questioned and some heads must roll. Witness the application of this same philosophy to athletic teams that end a string of successful seasons.

of the family budget and had required a different form of consumer purchasing—installment-payment purchasing. Housing, too, had become much more elaborate during the 1920s, and much more expensive. The increased investment in a residence had introduced changes in financing procedures, and under these a home owner would become obligated to continue payments for an ordinary residence over a period of twenty or more years.

These innovations (and there were many others) had contributed to the great expansion of business and industry in the 1920s, and had caused prosperity to be shared on the basis of a broad public participation. But when the business expansion collapsed, the resulting adversities simply had to affect a greater number of persons than ever before at a time of national financial catastrophe. The Depression involved many persons who did not have the slightest idea of what had happened to spoil their "good times." And, because at least some people were not completely impoverished, if seriously affected at all, there developed the somewhat absurd belief that those who were not suffering from the Depression had somehow instigated the crash and the deflation to further their own selfish motives.

Nevertheless, some Americans knew (and admitted at least to themselves) that their own shortcomings had contributed somehow to their personal depression plight. They showed this by what they did, no matter how they might have vocally attacked others for their dilemma. Quite a number of persons made the belated effort to develop a job skill, starting at the bottom wherever a menial job opportunity was available. Others scraped up the funds to resume an education that had been interrupted by their participation in the boom. Many small businessmen closed their shops, and sought employment wherever it might be available. And Americans generally learned for the first time in quite a number of years the difference between work that was real and work that was synthetic.

This review of the collapse of the "New Era" of the 1920s reveals how the American economy was restored to a state in which the inflation had been removed. By the year 1932, Americans understood once again that work effort, seriously and conscientiously applied, was needed to assure one's support. No longer were the delusions of support through "quick buck" gimmicks the order of the day. Americans, by and large, were ready to cooperate in restoring their economy to a level that would assure support for everyone, even though no one expected a return to the lush type of living that had marked the 1920s. To be lasting and durable, any new prosperity had to be structured without an overwhelming quantity of the inflation that had poisoned the prosperity of the just-departed "New Era."

Whether or not that goal could have been accomplished we shall never know, because at about the precise moment that the depression was hitting the bottom in 1932, a national election was required to be held. No one dedicated to the proposition of rebuilding a sounder American economy could have suggested that, with the confusion and bitterness prevalent in 1932, this would be an appropriate year for holding a presidential election. But this is what the law required.

Under the conditions then prevailing, it should have been a foregone conclusion that a national election could only produce the result of throwing the "ins" out of office. This meant, of course, that the then President of the United States, the late Herbert C. Hoover, stood little chance of being reelected. However, after the majority of Americans had expressed their vengeance by voting against Hoover, one should have anticipated that the citizens of the nation would thereafter face up to the greater problem of working cooperatively toward the rebuilding of a sound national economy. This had happened before in the case of other economic busts throughout American history. In each case there had been a closing of ranks and a temporary shelving of class hatreds while the people in the nation worked to rebuild a damaged economic structure. On the basis of this historical precedent, one should have expected that the government would adopt a "hands off" policy in matters economic, except to the extent of injecting such new laws as might prevent a recurrence of the evils that had cropped out during the boom that had collapsed.

But after the battle smoke of the 1932 election campaign had cleared, there was little possibility of a closing of the ranks, and even less opportunity for any cooperative effort in a rebuilding of the American economy. This was so because the 1932 election campaign

34

was the birthplace of a politically inspired economic class hatred that has continued to the present day. It is almost trite to suggest that all elections beginning with that of 1932 have not really involved a choice between candidates, or a choice between issues, but have involved a contest between classes. The warring factions have involved liberalism vs. conservatism; rich vs. poor; labor vs. capital; and theorists vs. businessmen. Party labels have become all but meaningless. Primarily, elections have reflected the process of the members of both political parties seeking to curry favor with the great bulk of American voters by advocating massive spending programs, presumably undertaken to help an allegedly poor class that has constantly increased in numbers in spite of any high level of business prosperity.

How this political philosophy reintroduced inflation into the American economy is the subject of succeeding chapters.

CHAPTER 3

How the Seeds of Inflation
Were Sown Again (1933–1939)

President Roosevelt, in the course of his campaigning for the Presidency in 1932, had singled out the overexpansion of the 1920s as the principal cause of the nation's economic difficulties. He had directed criticism at the overbuilding of American industrial plants, and the growth in corporate enterprise, particularly the increase in corporate surpluses. Of course, if the size of the American productive capacity was to be measured in terms of the reduced demand for products and services in 1932, one could readily join in the opinion that, temporarily at least, America's industrial plant had become overexpanded. However, Roosevelt did not limit his criticism about industrial overexpansion to the problem of plants standing idle because of depressed 1932 conditions. Instead, he claimed that the overexpansion exceeded a period of future growth. For example, in a Chicago speech of July 2, 1932, Roosevelt had said:

> In the years before 1929 we know that this country had completed a vast cycle of building and inflation; for ten years we expanded on the theory of repairing the wastes of the War, but actually expanding far beyond that, and also beyond our natural and normal growth. . . .

What was the result? Enormous corporate surpluses piled up—the most stupendous in history. Where, under the spell of delirious speculation, did those surpluses go? Let us talk economics that the figures prove and that we can understand. Why, they went chiefly in two directions, first, into new and unnecessary plants which now stand stark and idle; and second, into the call-money market of Wall Street, either directly by the corporations, or indirectly through the banks. Those are the facts. Why blink at them?

Then came the crash. You know the story. Surpluses invested in unnecessary plants became idle. . . .

And in a speech delivered at San Francisco on September 23, 1932, Roosevelt insisted that the problem confronting the nation in 1932 was not that of producing more goods. Instead, so he claimed, there had to be a better administration of the plants already built so as somehow to distribute wealth and products more equitably. This speech had included the following observation:

Our industrial plant is built; the problem just now is whether . . . it is not overbuilt. Our last frontier has long since been reached, and there is practically no more free land. . . . We are now providing a drab living for our own people. . . .
Our task now is not discovery or exploitation of natural resources, or necessarily producing more goods. It is the soberer, less dramatic business of administering resources and plants already in hand, of adjusting production to consumption, of distributing wealth and products more equitably.

Let us pause for a moment to reflect upon the meaning of the last portion of Roosevelt's quoted remarks, because these words actually provided a prophecy for the future. This becomes clear when we consider all that has happened in the forty years that have passed since the speech was offered. In his speech, Roosevelt was merely recommending that production be adjusted to consumption, and that wealth and products be distributed more equitably. Nothing too unusual about that suggestion for removing the customary fluctuations in an economy.

Nevertheless, this simple formula for an economy with fewer ups

37

and downs was later employed by Roosevelt as a national goal. Moreover, this goal became the standard for economic performance not only during Roosevelt's long tenure as President, but also during the terms of the Presidents that have succeeded him. And in applying that goal the Federal Government has become the biggest economic force in the world, because the Federal Government has constantly spent money to swell the national purchasing power, rather than to have purchasing power depend upon, and be identified with, productive activity. Those who have supported this goal have consistently emphasized the need for spending by all Americans as well as by the Government. There is hardly a single instance of an emphasis upon the need for productivity (and honest work effort) that has been taken for granted.

Perhaps Roosevelt's recommendation concerning an economic goal, when offered, seemed to provide a simple solution for the then-pressing problem of the reduced depression-level purchasing power (demand) being insufficient to absorb available goods (supply). In applying his solution, there was to be provided a more constant level of national purchasing power, which it later developed was to be supplied primarily with the aid of Government funds. Through making purchasing power more certain, it was assumed that you could avoid future depressions for all time, i.e., there could never be an excess of supply of goods over the demand for these, if sufficient purchasing power was always at hand. Unfortunately, however, as with all theories, this particular theory ignored the practical aspects.

When any people are supplied with an assured purchasing power, both the need and the incentive to improve the quantity and the quality of goods and services are eliminated. It was this very condition that caused the "image of plenty" psychology that had marked the 1920s. All that was needed to bring back this undesirable facet of mob psychology was for America to move out of the depression into more prosperous conditions. However, the possibility that such an application of the economic theory of assured purchasing power could of and by itself some day result in the greatest American inflation possible (i.e., an almost continuous excess of purchasing power over available goods) was considered most unlikely at the bottom depths of the Great Depression.

But we are getting ahead of our story.

The Roosevelt Administration started the planning of the economy at the very bottom of the Great Depression. This was a most propitious point of time to innovate on matters economic. The innovation obviously had to start out looking good, because the thoroughly deflated economy had no place to move except up, whether with or without any innovation. The closing of the nation's banks on the day Franklin Delano Roosevelt took office was a dramatic demonstration of slamming the door upon a prosperity that had already fled the scene. Hence, the only direction remaining for the national economy to take was up. Of course, there remained the question as to when and how the upward course would start, and this was coupled with some doubt as to the extent of any recovery from the depression lows.

The first order of business for the Roosevelt Administration was to establish government control over the nation's money. Without this the Government could not expect to control the economy. This was so, because since the dawn of civilization the people of almost any nation have been able to thwart the economic designs of those exercising political power by simply refusing to honor the money of the politicians. Traditionally, whenever a people had wanted to fight against the economic designs of their rulers, the people simply turned to using gold in their daily economic transactions. Once this took place, the politicians' paper soon became worthless. Back in the year 1933, any American could legally hold gold, gold coins or gold-backed currency, and a number of Americans had been in the habit of keeping a store of good money in safekeeping "just in case."

In order to advance his Government planning of the economy, Roosevelt had to eliminate the possibility of American citizens refusing to honor government-made paper money. He had to eliminate the process of citizens holding gold bonds, gold in bars, gold coins or gold-backed currency. Roosevelt decided that it was necessary for this nation to abandon the gold standard and devalue its currency. For this purpose, he reached back and revived a World War I emergency measure and used this as the basis for his Executive Order of April 5, 1933. This required all persons to take their gold, gold coins or gold-backed currency to their banks and exchange the gold for currency. The banks, in turn, were required to turn the gold and gold coins into the Federal Reserve Bank. Somewhat later, on January 30, 1934, the Presidential acts were given the dignity of more legality through Congress enacting the Gold Reserve Act. By still another action, Congress gave the President full legal authority to change the value of money (devalue money). This authority was contained in the so-called Thomas Amendment to the Agricultural Adjustment Act of May 12, 1933, which Senator Thomas himself described in the following words:

> Mr. President, it will be my task to show if the Amendment shall prevail it has potentialities as follows: It may transfer from one class to another class in these United States value to the extent of almost $200,000,000,000. This value will be transferred first from those who own the bank deposits; secondly, this value will be transferred from those who own bonds and fixed investments. If the Amendment carries and the powers are exercised in a reasonable degree, it must transfer that $200,000,000,000 in the hands of persons who now have it, who did not buy it, who did not earn it, who do not deserve it, who must not retain it, back to the other side, the debtor class of the Republic, the people who owe the mass debts of the nation.

So we find that before Congress was asked to rubber stamp some money legislation, Congress was being forewarned (perhaps politically "enticed" would be a more befitting description) by the conclusion that the legislation under consideration would transfer 200 billion dollars (in purchasing power) from the creditor class to the debtor class. Presumably, this satisfied the constitutional safeguard that prevented the taking of property without due process of law; i.e., the Senator who sponsored the new law simply concluded on his own that *those who were creditors did not deserve to own the property his law would confiscate!* Despite this bland admission that creditors who owned bonds and fixed investments were to be bilked by this legislation, this same Congress was working to protect with still other legislation many thousands of unsophisticated investors who had placed their life savings in fixed investments in the form of building and loan accounts, life insurance, mutual savings banks and real estate mortgage loans.

Apparently, these thrifty folks were among the creditors who did not deserve to own their life savings that the law would confiscate and turn over to the debtors.

Nevertheless, the United States Supreme Court approved of these procedures for debasing the currency in the Court's opinions in the "Gold Clause" cases. After the passage of the Gold Reserve Act, the price of gold was fixed at $35.00 per ounce instead of the $20.50 per ounce theretofore prevailing. And, of course, the whole purpose behind this repricing of gold, and the related laws and Executive Orders, was to raise prices—perhaps commodity prices in particular —by devaluating the purchasing power of the American dollar.

This manipulation of the currency was described by Budget Director Lewis Douglas (who resigned in August 1934) in rather blunt terminology:

> The Government, by its fiscal policies, has deliberately laid the base for another inflation on a scale so gigantic that the bubble of the 1920s may finally seem small by comparison. We are now evidently going to have bigger and more painful inflation under Government sponsorship and induced by direct Government action. The New Deal is only the former "New Era" dressed up in different clothes. When the next bubble bursts, let it not be forgotten that the responsibility lies directly at the door of the present Administration.

As is so often the case with economic forecasts that are proved accurate only after the passage of time, the results predicted by Budget Director Douglas did not take place immediately. The bursting of the 1929 bubble had been too severe, and the thorough deflation that followed could not immediately be reversed into a surge of inflation. However, viewing Douglas' forecast from the vantage point of the 1960s, we find his words to be nothing short of prophetic. And it is hoped that when, as and if the inflation bubble finally bursts, Douglas' words serve as a reminder of where to place the blame.

Moreover, in later chapters we shall learn how accurate Douglas had been in forecasting an inflation so gigantic that the bubble of the 1920s may seem small by comparison.

Contemporaneously with the establishment of government control over money, the Roosevelt Administration started economic planning. One of the first steps in the economic-planning process was the enactment of the National Industrial Recovery Act (NIRA) on June 16, 1933. The express purpose of this law was to control all economic transactions by having each industry, each trade group and each trade association become parties to codes of fair competition that had to be approved by the President of the United States. The NIRA followed customary bureaucratic procedures by giving the President supreme authority to administer the law, but with the actual administration to be delegated by the President to code agencies manned by numerous government employees. Once the NIRA was enacted, a businessman had no choice but to sign up under the appropriate code, otherwise he would have difficulty in continuing in business. However, if he did sign up under the appropriate Code division, he could proudly display the "Blue Eagle" as the insignia of his compliance and his patriotism. Thereafter, should he violate the dictates of the Code, he would be subject to fine and imprisonment.

The entire NIRA procedure was nothing short of a violation of antitrust laws, but under Government sponsorship. In practical application the NIRA restricted competition and encouraged the fixing of prices. And wages and practically everything else applicable to business were the subject of fixing, too. The theory behind the NIRA was to void the free-market conditions that were depressing wages and prices. However, on May 27, 1935, the United States Supreme Court decided that the NIRA was unconstitutional, and this grand experiment of the Federal Government, encouraging the fixing of prices and the restriction of competition, came to an abrupt end. There were quite a number of persons who held the belief, in 1935, that the Supreme Court had merely put the NIRA Blue Eagle out of its misery, because this experiment had been something less than successful. At least it could be said that this venture in the planning of the economy had not alleviated the depression conditions by much, if at all.

It could have been noted, too, that the NIRA had worked the greatest hardship upon those who were shopkeepers and the operators of small businesses. It had been the small business operators, and not the industrial giants, who had suffered under the iron hand of the allegedly expert NIRA administrators whose actions were seldom based upon any practical business experience. It was at this point of time that small business first learned about the difficulties in coping with big government. As a matter of fact, the administration of the NIRA set the pattern for all subsequent incursions of the Federal Government into the realm of controlling business procedures. The NIRA set the pattern, too, for encouraging a bigness in business that has continued to the present time. This is to say that bureaucratic government administrators breed bureaucratic subjects for such administration.

It has been mentioned how Congress debased the currency to relieve debtors. This was not the only legislative approach toward aiding those who owed money. Congress also enacted an amendment to the Federal Bankruptcy Law (the amendment bore the label "Section 77B"). This was intended to facilitate the reorganizations of corporations and other debtors that were unable to meet their debts. It had been intended that this legislation would minimize the customary delays and reduce the heavy legal expense ordinarily associated with regular bankruptcy proceedings, so as to contribute toward reducing the losses in property values ordinarily associated with a bankruptcy proceeding. Nevertheless, there is substantial ground for believing that these reorganization procedures did nothing more than to aid the debtors (stockholders) at the expense of the many hundreds of thousands of the nation's unsophisticated thrifty who had purchased "first mortgage gold bonds" in the boomtime 1920s only to learn that the interest payments on these bonds stopped about as soon as the dust of the 1929 stock market crash had settled. And when the disillusioned bondholders had to sell their defaulted bonds at ten and twenty cents on the dollar to raise money,

43

the bonds were often purchased by persons identified with the debtor (the shareholders). Proof of the fact that the rights of small bondholders were often neglected in the reorganization proceedings under Section 77B lies in the fact that, not too long after Section 77B was enacted, it was found necessary to authorize the Securities & Exchange Commission to pass upon and approve many types of re-organization plans. Otherwise the small bondholders might have suffered even greater losses.

Congress also enacted laws intended to change and correct the economic practices that had contributed in building the boom-bust pattern that had exploded. These laws were released on a mass-production basis. For example, laws were enacted to control the issuance of securities as well as transactions in securities; to insure deposits in banks; to insure investments in mutual building associa-tions, including a new form of Federally chartered "Savings and Loan Associations"; and to provide benefit payments during unem-ployment and Social Security benefits during retirement.

When passed by Congress in the early 1930s, these economic con-trol laws were practically deified by quite a number of well-meaning persons. However, a more objective analysis of this flood of new laws should have suggested that too much law was being applied too late. The entire process could have been described as putting a halter on a horse to prevent his running away—*at the precise time when the horse had fallen to the ground in sheer exhaustion after having already run away.* That this hobbling of the economy with control laws could accomplish nothing more during the 1930s than to help keep an already deflated economy at depression levels should have been obvious.

How was the American economy hobbled by these economic con-trol laws? By making practically all business and financial trans-actions more difficult to accomplish and far more expensive. A new cost factor of vast importance was introduced through the bureau-cratic control over day-to-day transactions that required a regular reading of laws and regulations, the accumulation of large quantities of statistics, and the regular filing of forms with governmental au-thorities. Of course, initially, during the depression, this emphasis upon paper work was only started. Later, during World War II and thereafter, it was expanded by leaps and bounds. These innovations gave to the members of the accounting and legal professions an essential role in the conduct of practically all business and finance.

Who had to bear these added costs of doing business? Eventually the consumer, of course. However, during the period of the depression it was difficult for business to increase prices so as to "pass on" the new costs to the consumer. But once the depression difficulties associated with increasing prices were removed (this happened during World War II and thereafter), prices had to skyrocket as businessmen were able to increase prices to compensate for the added costs incurred through compliance with the economic control legislation. Obviously, the control legislation was another factor that paved the way for a new inflation: this legislation brought into the business and financial arenas a large number of persons who had little to do with the production of goods and services, or bringing these to the consumer; the compensation paid these persons had to increase the costs of goods and services; and eventually (when prices could be increased) this added cost would be reflected in higher prices.

After the depression had run its course, the original purpose of many of these laws was forgotten, which caused the law to accomplish an entirely different purpose at some later date. This can best be demonstrated by a reference to the depression-bred law that required time-and-a-half pay for work in excess of forty hours per week. When this law came into being during the depression, it had the obvious purpose of spreading employment by penalizing employers with an added labor cost whenever they required an employee to work more than forty hours per week. However, during World War II there was a scarcity rather than an overabundance of employable persons, and there certainly was no need for spreading employment by penalizing employers for employing persons more than forty hours per week. Nevertheless, neither during World War II nor during the boom that followed, was the law changed. And employers had to pay the extra 50 percent of compensation in every instance for all hours worked in excess of the forty-hours-per-week standard of the depression. The application of this law tremendously

45

increased the cost to the Government (and to the taxpayers) of financing World War II, and thereafter increased the cost of all products and services for the consumer. It stands to reason that the employment hours covered by this overtime pay are no more productive than the regular forty hours that can be worked without the overtime pay. Hence, this extra labor cost is inflation pure and simple. Unfortunately, when the economic experts complain how inflation has increased prices, they never mention the excellent example of how this particular law has contributed to inflation.

Hobbled with restrictive laws, it should have caused no surprise that business and finance were barely able to move much above the depression lows during the entire period of the 1930s. This condition can be corroborated by noting the movements of the Dow Jones Industrial Stock Average that, as previously mentioned, had recovered from its July 1932 low, only to slump later to 50.16 immediately before the bank holiday and the inauguration of President Roosevelt in early March 1933. Thereafter, under the influence of politically inspired enthusiasm (and the reopening of the banks) the Dow Jones Industrial Average promptly moved upward to 108.67 by July 1933. However, the Average then moved sidewise for the balance of the year 1933, throughout all of the year 1934 and during the spring of 1935. The movement of this stock average reflected the period of watching and waiting while the economic control legislation literally poured out of the Halls of Congress, and while the experiment of government-sponsored cartelism under the National Industrial Recovery Act was getting under way.

The completely obvious stalemate for business, as reflected in this stock market price index, terminated abruptly in May 1935. This was when the Supreme Court determined that the NIRA was unconstitutional. Practically overnight, there occurred an immediate revival of interest in business and in the stock market. The resulting business recovery was very much in evidence during the balance of 1935, and the business improvement gained momentum during 1936 and early 1937. As business improved, prices and wages rose from the depression depths without the help of any government sponsorship. The Dow Jones Industrial Stock Average promptly acknowledged the obvious improvement in the economy after the NIRA had been abolished by increasing from the 100 level (a position that it had occupied since mid-1933) to 148.44 by November 1935, and on up to the 180–190 level by November 1936.

These signs of improvement in the national economy during 1935–1936 were considered by many persons as the surest indication that the depression emergency was at long last on the way out. Quite a number of business leaders expected that the government attempts to control the economy would terminate, too; that is, except for the continued administration of the many new control laws. But President Roosevelt and his inner circle of advisors were not about to admit that the emergency was over, at least they were not inclined to release the economy from their grip. This became evident in the struggle between the national administration and the business and financial community. And this controversy came into the open and attained notoriety when it was extended into the political arena. There it reached the boiling point in President Roosevelt's highly publicized feud with the United States Supreme Court. President Roosevelt blamed the Supreme Court for the collapse of his plan of a government-controlled economic recovery, and he did not intend to admit that the economy could recover without government sponsorship. Apparently Roosevelt concluded, too, that, no matter what the leaders of business and finance or the Supreme Court might happen to think about his planning of the economy, it so happened that the electorate had reelected him Chief Executive in 1936.

It became obvious that when President Roosevelt lost the support of many of his former advisors and political associates, he decided to go it alone. And he "threw down the gauntlet" in a most dramatic fashion when, on April 2, 1937, he reminded those in command of the nation's business that he, and he alone, knew what was good for the economy. On that particular day, he openly attacked the excessive prices for durable goods, singling out a boost in copper prices for special criticism. The President's attack on prices, in the midst of a somewhat modest recovery in business, stunned the business community. Prior to that time, Roosevelt had been openly advocating increases in prices and wages to restore business and employment to

47

above-depression levels. As a matter of fact, a government-sponsored restoration of prices to at least profitable levels had been one of the principal objectives of the NIRA. And after that law had been held unconstitutional by the Supreme Court, prices and wages had promptly improved without government help.

The shock of President Roosevelt's April 2, 1937, attack upon prices was immediately reflected in Wall Street. Stock prices stopped the upward movement that had started with real vigor upon the demise of the NIRA and, during the summer of 1937, business activity was again stalemated in an atmosphere of cautious watching and waiting so reminiscent of the 1933–1935 years. The only remnant of the 1935–1936 optimism that remained in the summer of 1937 was the oft-repeated phrase that "things will open up after Labor Day." However, that expectation proved futile, because the day after Labor Day, 1937, stock prices suffered a severe collapse and a drop in business activity followed almost immediately thereafter. Although President Roosevelt employed extreme care in labeling the termination of the 1935–1937 boomlet as a "recession" (rather than a depression), there were quite a number of persons who privately held the belief that the Great Depression had merely been interrupted by the 1935–1937 improvement. Hence these persons believed that in the fall of 1937 the depression was all set to resume its course. The 1938 "recession" bottomed in 1938 and, by March 1938, the Dow Jones Industrial Stock Average had again sunk down to the 100 level, where it had been before the NIRA had been abolished.

President Roosevelt's April 2, 1937, attack upon prices has somehow escaped historical recognition, even though it was an important event in American economic history. From that day forward, it has been no novelty for a President of the United States himself to decide what is best for the economy, without bothering to have laws enacted by Congress and without waiting for laws to be interpreted by the United States Supreme Court. Since April 2, 1937, several Presidents have employed the approach of having their own economic views broadly broadcast to still all opposition, even though the bones of those who signed the Declaration of Independence and those who labored to formulate the United States Constitution must have rattled in their graves.

If President Roosevelt's April 2, 1937, diatribe against prices was primarily intended to quell the rebirth of speculation that had followed the demise of his beloved NIRA, he was entirely successful. After his publicized attack on prices there occurred an immediate decline in the monthly dollar volume of shares traded on the New York Stock Exchange, starting with the precise month (April 1937) when President Roosevelt had delivered his attack against high prices. Here are the telltale statistics.

TABLE 3

1937	Money Value of Shares Traded New York Stock Exchange (in billions of dollars)	1937	Money Value of Shares Traded New York Stock Exchange (in billions of dollars)
January	2.24	July	1.09
February	2.33	August	.98
March	2.61	September	1.43
April	1.80	October	1.64
May	1.11	November	1.22
June	.87	December	1.11

Source: New York Stock Exchange published data.

Although the money value of shares traded increased slightly thereafter, beginning with the month of September 1937, this particular increase had merely accompanied the downward plunge in share prices. As a matter of fact, the money value of shares traded experienced for the entire year 1936 (before the President's April 2, 1937, attack upon prices) *was never again equaled throughout the balance of President Roosevelt's long term of office as President.* Table 4 proves this statement.

There could be no better demonstration of the economic power of one particular Chief Executive of the United States than is reflected in these share-trading statistics. Roosevelt had effectively put an end to increased levels of stock trading for the balance of his lifetime.

When stripped of political considerations, President Roosevelt's clashes with the business and financial community, his feuds with his fellow politicians and his battles with the United States Supreme

TABLE 4

Year	Money Value of Shares Traded New York Stock Exchange (in billions of dollars)	Year	Money Value of Shares Traded New York Stock Exchange (in billions of dollars)
1936	20.366*	1941	2.253
1937	18.433	1942	3.673
1938	11.013	1943	7.670
1939	9.968	1944	8.252
1940	7.166		

Source: New York Stock Exchange published data.

*The 1936 dollar volume of New York Stock Exchange share trades was never again exceeded until 1954 when Dwight D. Eisenhower (a Republican) was President. For 1954 the volume was above $24 billion. In that same year of 1954, the Dow Jones Industrial Average equaled and then surpassed its 1929 high for the first time since 1929.

Court had represented nothing more than the course of Roosevelt pursuing his campaign promises. Roosevelt and his inner sanctum of economic advisors simply did not believe that the American economy could function properly without government supervision of one sort or another. They refused to accept an uncontrolled economy that they believed could only develop into the conditions of overspeculation and overexpansion that had marked the late 1920s. The immediate upsurge in business and in speculative activity that had followed the death of the NIRA in 1935 had been completely contrary to Roosevelt's plan for a status-quo-type economy. Roosevelt was insisting that the American economy was to move on an even keel without sporadic ups and downs, and he did not hesitate to use the power of the Federal Government to enforce his beliefs.

There is evidence available that demonstrates how the economy was in fact kept at a status quo (frozen position) condition by the Roosevelt Administration. For example, in his campaign speeches, Roosevelt had attacked the overexpansion in corporate surpluses and the overexpansion in productive plants. These not only failed to increase, but they in fact decreased during the Roosevelt Administration until the start of World War II.

50

Considering first America's productive plant, information taken from the Federal income tax returns filed by all corporations for the period 1930–1939, inclusive, reveals that the reported total of fixed (or capital) assets less depreciation (and this really means plant and equipment in most cases) declined most perceptibly. This is demonstrated by the following index (computed with the tax-return figures for 1935 serving as 100 percent):

TABLE 5

INDEX OF FIXED ASSETS LESS DEPRECIATION
OF ALL CORPORATIONS FILING
FEDERAL INCOME TAX RETURNS
(1935 = 100%)

1930	120.42%	1935	100.00%
1931	113.76	1936	97.41
1932	108.03	1937	99.84
1933	104.46	1938	98.82
1934	102.26	1939	99.75

Source: Computations made from data supplied by Internal Revenue publications.

Somewhat similarly, the capital stock and accumulated surplus reported by all corporations filing Federal income tax returns also failed to increase from just about the time that Roosevelt took office until the start of World War II. This is demonstrated by the following index (again the return figures for 1935 are computed as 100 percent):

TABLE 6

INDEX OF TOTAL CAPITAL AND SURPLUS
OF ALL CORPORATIONS FILING
FEDERAL INCOME TAX RETURNS
(1935 = 100%)

1930	116.09%	1935	100.00%
1931	103.19	1936	96.07
1932	96.14	1937	101.94
1933	91.83	1938	98.92
1934	101.91	1939	98.51

Source: Computations made from data supplied by Internal Revenue publications.

Unfortunately, the American economy could not furnish job opportunities under the condition of declining investments in corporate productive plants and frozen corporate capital structures. Employment had increased after the Supreme Court eliminated the NIRA, but when President Roosevelt unleashed his attack upon prices, the improvement in employment was reversed. These conditions were clearly revealed in the unemployment statistics:

TABLE 7

TOTAL UNEMPLOYED PERSONS
DURING THE GREAT DEPRESSION

Year	Unemployed (stated in millions)	Year	Unemployed (stated in millions)
1930	4.34	1935	10.61
1931	8.02	1936	9.03
1932	12.06	1937	7.70
1933	12.83	1938	10.39
1934	11.34	1939	9.48

Sources: Bureau of the Census;
Bureau of Labor Statistics.

Since a shackled economy could not furnish sufficient jobs or provide sufficient income to support the American people, Roosevelt and his advisors had to find another source of income to help support the economy. This was easy to accomplish. The Roosevelt Administration determined that a depression was an emergency just like a war. Hence what could be more logical than to collect taxes and spend government money during a depression as during a war? And the depression-period tax collections soon outstripped those collected for World War I years, as the data, computed on a June 30th collection year basis, reveal in Table 8.

Nevertheless, although tax collections skyrocketed, the Federal Government depression-period expenditures continued to exceed even the increased tax collections. So we find that although total private debt declined during the depression, the total of Federal debt increased, as demonstrated in Table 9.

The process of increasing Federal tax collections while the

52

TABLE 8

FEDERAL TAX COLLECTION COMPARISONS
FOR DIFFERENT YEARS

	Year	Collections in Billions of Dollars
Internal Revenue	1917	$0.8 billion
collections identified	1918	3.7 "
with World War I expenditures	1919	3.8 "
	1920	5.4 "
	1921	4.6 "
Internal Revenue collections, 1922–1930, inclusive		2.852 billion average per year
Internal Revenue collections during the Great Depression	1931	2.4 "
	1932	1.6 "
	1933	1.6 "
	1934	2.7 "
	1935	3.3 "
	1936	3.5 "
	1937	4.7 "
	1938	5.7 "
	1939	5.2 "

Source: Internal Revenue published statistics.

TABLE 9

FEDERAL GOVERNMENT DEBT vs. PRIVATE DEBT,
SELECTED YEARS

Year	Total Private Debt	Federal Debt
	(billions of dollars)	
1929	88.1	16.5
1933	81.9	24.3
1939	76.0	42.6

Source: Department of Commerce.

economy was depressed required a new approach in collecting taxes. This was accomplished by completely changing the original intent and purpose of the Federal income tax law so as to subject even the earnings of the workers to an income tax. I will explain in the next

53

chapter how this was done. However, before proceeding to that chapter let me reemphasize that the seeds of inflation sown by the Roosevelt Administration during the Great Depression were not recognized as such, because it was impossible for purchasing power, even though artificially inflated, to exceed the available supply of goods and services at that time.

CHAPTER 4

The Perversion of the Income Tax
(1932-1945)

The preceding chapter mentioned how the Federal Government had increased its spending during the Great Depression. Part of the funds for this had been obtained through increasing the Federal debt. Nevertheless, as that chapter also explained, Internal Revenue collections in the years beginning with 1935 had actually exceeded the tax collections during the period 1918–1921, when the cost of World War I was being financed.

Confronted with the need for finding a source of funds for Federal spending during the depression, those in government turned to the income tax to accomplish this purpose. However, the income tax law at that time was really unusable to collect massive amounts of taxes, because it had been structured primarily to "soak the rich." It might be well to pause and explain how that term, "soak the rich," came into being, because without that explanation it will be difficult to describe how changes in the income tax law have provided the greatest source of inflation.

When the income tax was born, it was designed to be assessed *primarily* upon income from accumulated wealth in the form of stocks and bonds. Obviously, only the "rich" could have income from accumulated wealth. To find the original meaning of the words "soak the rich," one must search through portions of the *Congressional Record* of 1909 and that of 1913.

Such a search will reveal that, from the time that the Sixteenth (income tax) Amendment was born in 1909, Congress respected the fact that in order to restrict the tax-soaking process to the rich it was necessary to provide a relatively large annual tax exemption. This would make certain that the more modest amounts of income that were obtained by working for a living (in the form of wages or salaries) would escape completely the new income tax. Further, in designing the new income tax Congress also acknowledged that the tax rate applying to large amounts of income from accumulated wealth had to be kept low. Otherwise, it was suspected that the income tax would simply be "passed on" by the rich to other, and less wealthy, segments of the economic community.* As a matter of fact, in their deliberations about the new income tax at the time that it was originally adopted, the members of Congress acknowledged, too, that any income tax assessed against the incomes of corporations, or those in business, would simply be passed on as costs of doing business, and included with the prices the consumer had to pay.

Now, during the Great Depression it would have been completely unrealistic to expect to raise large amounts of income taxes under a law that was restricted to "soaking the rich." At that time there were very few persons with substantial incomes in the form of interest and dividends from accumulated wealth. Accordingly, if large amounts of taxes were to be raised through an application of the income tax, the law had to be changed. Obviously, the change had to involve the process of taxing the more modest amounts of income, and these consisted primarily of the salaries and wages of the workers.

This same procedure had been followed once before in order for the Government to raise extraordinary amounts of taxes—when it was required to finance the heavy costs of World War I. However,

---

*As a matter of fact, prior to the income tax the Government was supported primarily by tariffs. And high tariffs simply meant higher prices for the consumer. This is a result that the income tax was supposed to avoid by restricting its application to the rich.

after World War I the Federal income tax law had been restored for the most part to its original intent of collecting taxes primarily from the income realized from accumulated wealth. For example, in 1929 (when the Republicans were in office) a husband and wife having $5,000 of taxable income (before exemptions) paid a Federal income tax of only $10.00. And a $5,000 annual income in 1929 represented a tidy sum in terms of purchasing power.

There were two changes in the tax law that were needed if the income tax was to reach out and tax the more modest amounts of income, as well as to raise much greater amounts in annual tax revenues than ever before. The first of these steps was to decrease the annual exemptions, and the second was perceptibly to increase the tax rates. However, to undertake these two steps was political suicide, since this would affect the general public, that is the majority of the voters. To overcome this political difficulty, any changes in the income tax law had to continue the illusion that the tax "soaked the rich," even though Congress knew that after the law was changed most taxes would be collected from persons that were not rich.

Hence, Congress had to initiate a third change in the tax law, and this was to impose confiscatory tax rates upon high amounts of income. Only by this process could the illusion be continued that the income tax "soaked the rich."* There is no other conclusion but that the confiscatory tax rates on high incomes serve only a political purpose.

The process of changing the income tax law from its original intent started in 1932 even before the Roosevelt Administration took office. The annual surtax exemption for a husband and wife was reduced from $10,000 to $6,000, and the annual normal tax exemption from $3,500 to $2,500. Of course, these amounts still represented rela-

*As a matter of fact, the confiscatory tax rates applied to large amounts of income do not in truth "soak the rich," because most of the taxpayers with large amounts of income are not rich, i.e., they do not have accumulated wealth. Rather, these large incomes for the most part have been earned by working for a living, whether as employees or self-employed. On the other hand, those with accumulated wealth could follow a course to avoid completely, or at least minimize, the income tax, such as through realizing income in the form of municipal bond interest, or from oil ventures, or as capital gains. However, this explanation has seldom, if ever, been given adequate publicity.

57

tively high annual incomes in terms of purchasing power during the depression era of low prices. Simultaneously with the reduction of the annual exemptions, the income tax rates were perceptibly increased, particularly so for the larger amounts of annual income.

However, the outbreak of World War II presented the opportunity to Congress completely to ignore any political hazard in taxing low amounts of income. Every American had to expect to help pay for his own defense. As a matter of fact, Congress did not even wait until America became a war participant, but started a year earlier, in 1941, to tax the incomes of every worker. In 1941, the annual surtax exemption was reduced to $1,500, and tax rates were shoved upward. By successive amendments to the tax law during the war, the rates were increased additionally. In 1945, the annual exemption was reduced to $1,000 for husband and wife. And the war emergency introduced the withholding tax so as to assure a prompt collection of taxes from the workers. This was the last step needed to make certain that the income tax would be an indirect (hidden) tax rather than a direct tax (this will be explained later). Meanwhile, however, the "soak the rich" image was steadfastly retained by applying confiscatory rates to high levels of income.

The decrease in the annual income tax exemption from the $20,-000 that applied in 1916 to the $1,200 applicable since 1948 represented quite a drop. However, to get a better idea as to the magnitude of the drop in the annual exemption, it should be expressed in dollars identical of purchasing power, i.e., the exemption should be stated on a constant dollar basis. Using the purchasing power of the dollar in 1967 as the measurement, Table 10 shows what happened to the exemption.

Meanwhile, however, the politicians in both of the major political parties have sanctimoniously proclaimed their concern for the plight of the small-income earner, and they have demonstrated their concern by unleashing one multi-billion-dollar spending program after another to relieve the plight of the "underprivileged." And when, on occasion, some voter has questioned the horrendous cost of these programs to the taxpayers, he has been reminded that for the most part the money is paid out of income taxes that "soak the rich."

58

TABLE 10

FEDERAL INCOME TAX SURTAX EXEMPTION FOR
SPECIFIC YEARS, CONVERTED TO CONSTANT DOLLARS

	Actual Annual Surtax Exemption— Husband and Wife	Consumer Price Index 1967 = 100	Surtax Exemption Converted Into 1967 Dollars
1916	$20,000	32.7	$61,162
1920	5,000	60.0	8,333
1925	10,000	52.5	19,048
1928	10,000	51.3	19,493
1933	6,000	38.8	15,464
1939	6,500	41.6	15,625
1941	1,500	44.1	3,401
1945	1,000	53.9	1,855
1950	1,200	72.1	1,664
1955	1,200	80.2	1,496
1960	1,200	88.7	1,353
1966	1,200	97.2	1,235
1967	1,200	100.0	1,200
1968	1,200	104.2	1,152
1969	1,200	109.8	1,093

Sources: (1) Surtax exemption as per Internal Revenue Code.
(2) Price index from Bureau of Labor Statistics.

It is, of course, difficult to understand how the income tax law could "soak the rich" in 1969 in the same manner as it did in 1916 (50+ years earlier) when the annual tax exemption in terms of 1969 purchasing power of the dollar had collapsed—from $61,162 in 1916 to $1,093 in 1969. Hence, rather than accept at face value the popular cliche of the politicians concerning the income tax, let us examine the facts. These are available in the form of published statistics of the U. S. Treasury Department (Internal Revenue Service).

The statistics clearly reveal how each decrease in the annual tax exemption has caused an immediate increase in the salaries and wages portion of total personal income reported for tax purposes. In 1933, even as during World War I, salaries and wages accounted for more than 50 percent of the total income reported to Internal Revenue. And the reductions in the tax exemption during World War II caused the salary and wage earners to account for ever larger proportions of total personal (noncorporate) taxable income. Here are the facts:

TABLE 11

HOW THE DECREASE IN TAX EXEMPTIONS HAS CAUSED TO
INCREASE THE "SALARY AND WAGES" PROPORTION OF
TOTAL INCOME REPORTED

	Salaries & Wages as % of Personal Income Reported	Surtax Exemption, Husband and Wife	Normal Tax Exemption
1916	22.2%	$20,000	$4,000
1920	57.4	5,000	2,000
1925	38.6	10,000	2,500
1928	37.7	10,000	3,500
1933	57.1	6,000	2,500
1939	63.4	6,500	2,500
1941	74.1	1,500	1,500
1945	76.2	1,000	1,000
1950	77.3	1,200	1,200
1955	80.4	1,200	1,200
1960	81.8	1,200	1,200
1965	80.9	1,200	1,200
1968	81.4	1,200	1,200

Source: Computed from Internal Revenue statistics of income reports for various
        years.

Obviously, the income from accumulated wealth that is the income of the rich had to become an insignificant portion of the total income that was taxed. The next tabulation demonstrates this.

The manner in which the drop in tax exemptions caused the rich no longer to supply major proportions of total income tax revenues can also be the subject of proof. Bear in mind that, in this instance, we are talking about the proportions of total personal income taxes paid by the rich as opposed to the proportion of total personal income taxes that was paid by the rich when the income tax law started in operation. The proof starts with the valid assumption that anyone having $100,000 and more of income in 1916 was truly rich, that is he did not get such a large amount of income by working for a living. Accordingly, since taxpayers with $100,000 or more of income paid

TABLE 12

TAXABLE INCOME OF INDIVIDUALS BY
PRINCIPAL CLASSES OF INCOME REPORTED

| Income Classification | % in Classification to Total Individual Income Reported | |
	1916	1968
Salaries and Wages	22.2%	81.4%
Dividends and Interest	25.6%	5.8%*
All other classes	52.2%	12.8%*
	100.0%	100.0%

Source: Computed from Internal Revenue statistics of income reports for years stated.

*This is the income of the rich that the Sixteenth Amendment was originally intended to tax.

73.1 percent of the total personal Federal income taxes in 1916, it is obvious that at that period the rich paid by far the greatest proportion of the total personal income taxes. Now, of course, we cannot make the same assumption for the more recent year of 1968; that is to say that anyone with $100,000 or more of income in 1968 was not necessarily rich; and most likely some of such taxpayers with large incomes obtained them from working. Nevertheless, for the year 1968, those with $100,000 or more of income contributed only 9.2 percent of the total Federal personal income taxes paid for that year. Further, in 1968, persons with less than the relatively modest amount of $20,000 of income contributed 65.5 percent of the total Federal personal income taxes collected. The complete tabulation is in Table 13.

Confronted with this evidence that it is primarily the workers, and not the rich, that support the Federal Government bureaucracy, the politicians are apt to explain that in 1968 the rich (who by that year were often workers in high-income brackets) were soaked at much higher tax rates. This is true. However, while the politicians are in an explaining mood, they might also explain why those with less than $3,000 of income had their modest incomes taxed at almost the same rate in 1968 as the rate applied to the rich in 1916. Yes, those with incomes of $3,000 and less in 1968 paid total taxes representing 6.47

61

TABLE 13

TABLE OF INCOME TAX LIABILITY
REPORTED BY INCOME CLASSES

| Income Bracket | The Tax Contribution of Different Brackets of Incomes to Total Individual Tax Payments | |
	1916	1968
Less than $ 3,000	0.0%	1.6%
$ 3,000 – $ 5,000	0.5%	4.5%
$ 5,000 – $ 10,000	3.6%	23.4%
$10,000 – $ 25,000	6.7%	N.A.
$10,000 – $ 20,000	N.A.	36.0%
$25,000 – $100,000	16.1%	N.A.
$20,000 – $100,000	N.A.	25.3%
Over $100,000	73.1%	9.2%
	100.0%	100.0%

Source: Computed from Internal Revenue statistics of income reports for various years.

percent of the total income reported in that bracket, whereas in 1916 the rich with $100,000 and more of income paid a total tax that accounted for only 6.8 percent of the total income reported in that bracket for that year. A complete tabulation is in Table 14.

Meanwhile, those with modest amounts of income have been "strung along" with an occasional promise that their tax plight will some day be eased by an increase in the annual tax exemption. That this is a promise that is not apt to be fulfilled becomes clear upon looking at some figures supplied by the *Glenn Davis Digest* of March 17, 1969 (issued by Congressman Glenn Davis of Wisconsin). According to Congressman Davis, even minor increases in the annual exemption would cause tremendous losses in annual income tax revenues (see Table 15).

The process of placing the income tax burden upon the American workers provided the Federal Government with a most reliable source of annual tax revenues. After the change in the income tax law had been completed during World War II, the Government could collect the great bulk of its revenues from many millions of workers with relatively modest incomes. Properly analyzed, however, this

TABLE 14

TABLE OF EFFECTIVE TAX RATES
BY INCOME CLASSES

Income Bracket	% of Taxes Paid to Adjusted Gross Income for Each Bracket	
	1916	1968
Less than $ 3,000	0.0%	6.47%
$ 3,000 – $ 5,000	0.125%	8.96%
$ 5,000 – $ 10,000	0.610%	10.52%
$10,000 – $ 25,000	0.945%	N.A.
$10,000 – $ 20,000	N.A.	13.37%
$25,000 – $100,000	1.81%	N.A.
$20,000 – $100,000	N.A.	22.28%
Over $100,000	6.80%	42.10%

Source: Computed from Internal Revenue statistics of income reports for various
years.

TABLE 15

EFFECT ON TAX COLLECTIONS OF MINOR
INCREASES IN PERSONAL EXEMPTIONS

Annual Increase in Personal Exemptions	Estimated Annual Decrease in Tax Collections
$100.00	3.6 billion dollars
400.00	12.0 ″ ″
600.00	17.3 ″ ″

Source: *Glenn Davis Digest* of March 17, 1969.

taxing process had to take spending money (i.e., the taxes collected)
from the workers, and turn this spending money over to the Federal
Government. This had to deprive the worker of funds for purchasing,
as well as money for saving.

Of course, the Government would have this same tax money for
Government spending purposes. Nevertheless, the employment of
these funds by the Government was not the same as when these
funds were in the hands of the workers. The Government's spending
would be for purposes generally unrelated to the production of goods
and services wanted and needed by consumers. On the other hand,

63

had the workers retained the dollars taken from them as income taxes, these would have been spent by the workers for goods and services. In fact, even the portion of these tax dollars that might have been saved by the workers would have contributed to building the capital structure of the private sector of the economy.

Obviously, the funneling of this money from private to Government spending increased nonproductive Government activity at the expense of activity in the private sector of the economy that could have been expected to increase the production of goods and services. Hence, the Government's spending of part of the workers' compensation collected as taxes would serve to increase the supply of money and credit, without at the same time increasing the available supply of goods and services. That this would inflate the economy, i.e., cause the spending of money (the demand) to exceed the available goods and services (the supply) should have been acknowledged.

Of course, the taking of the tax money from the workers could be expected to cause the workers to reduce their spending, since they had fewer dollars to spend after paying the taxes. But the belt-tightening process did not last. This brings up the point recognized by Congress when the income tax was born and the rich were to be soaked. At that time a low rate of tax had been applied to the large incomes from accumulated wealth so as to give little incentive to the "rich" to pass on their income tax to other segments of the community. However, the tax rates were greatly increased during the Depression, and again during World War II, and if the opportunity were available, it should have been expected that this tax burden would be passed on to others, wherever possible, by the payers of the tax.

Bear in mind that if the worker could pass on the tax, there would be no need for any belt tightening. And the worker was able to do just that. By obtaining increased wages or salaries, he was able to pass on his income tax burden to his employer. The employer could in turn pass on the worker's tax burden (higher wage and salary costs), together with the employer's own tax burden, to the customers of the employer in the form of increased prices.

Let us bear in mind, too, however, that when the first installment of the greatly increased income tax burden was introduced during the depression, workers could not get wage or salary increases, nor could businessmen increase prices. That is, not if the worker wanted to keep his job, or the businessman wanted to continue to have customers. Then when the second installment of the tax burden was loaded upon workers and those in business, during World War II, there again had been no opportunity to increase wages or prices. This time there was a different obstacle—salaries and prices were "frozen" for the most part by law.

Hence, during the long period of time when the new income tax burdens were being placed into effect, i.e., during the depression and during World War II, these tax burdens had to be borne directly by those that paid the increased taxes. The increased income taxes could not be passed on from worker to employer, and then from employer to customer. However, the removal of wage, salary and price freezing after the close of World War II presented that opportunity. Then, for the first time in years, the workers could get more compensation to cover their income tax, and American business could obtain higher prices to cover both the higher compensation paid to employees because of the income tax, and the businessman's part of the income tax. Equally important, workers were at that time hard to get, and products were in short supply, so that it was not difficult to increase wages, salaries and prices.

That the opportunity to increase wages, salaries and prices was used to pass the income tax burden on to the consumer is demonstrated by the increases in prices and wages (and, of course, salaries too) that took place as soon as the freezing restrictions were eliminated on or about the year 1946. The evidence is in Table 16.

However, this process of passing on income taxes in the form of increased prices was simply labeled "inflation." And, closely analyzed, it really was inflation, because the huge Federal Government expenditures contributed next to nothing in making available goods and services (the supply), yet at the same time these same Government expenditures had to kite the amount of purchasing power in the form of money and credit (the demand). Let us recall here that the dictionary definition explains inflation as being an ex-

TABLE 16

INCREASES IN PRICES AND WAGES AFTER THE
ELIMINATION OF WORLD WAR II PRICE AND WAGE FREEZING
(Average Straight-Time Hourly Earnings
of Production Workers in Manufacturing)

Year	Monthly Average		Consumer Price Index
	Gross	Excluding Overtime	
1943	$ .957	$ .881	60.3
1944	1.011	.933	61.3
1945	1.016	.949	62.7
1946	1.075	1.035	68.0
1947	1.217	1.18	77.8
1948	1.328	1.29	83.8

Source: Bureau of Labor Statistics.

cess of money and credit (purchasing power) over the available supply of goods.

And as the Government continued to tax and spend, first wages and salaries, and then prices, moved upward in wave after wave. Unfortunately, the very name applied to this development, i.e., the Wage-Price Spiral, served to hide the basic cause. The name should have been Tax-Price Spiral, or even more appropriate, the Government Spending-Price Spiral.

In reality, one of the old and forgotten laws of economics had taken over the chore of forcing Americans *either* to produce sufficient goods to equal the purchasing power that had been artificially increased by Government spending on nonproductive pursuits, *or* to suffer the consequences in the form of higher prices. This was a sophisticated version of the belt tightening that is required every time too many members of any society are engaged in work activity having little relation to the production of goods and services needed and wanted for human survival and support. Unfortunately, under the condition that the Federal Government had a sort of pipeline to the workers' pay checks, the chain of successive increases in wages and prices could not readily be broken.

Meanwhile, no one bothered to explain to the American workers that they could not win the game of passing on the income tax. For one thing, all workers are consumers, and as consumers they had to pay the higher prices as these were inflated to include the income tax burdens. Secondly, the prices would become inflated to include the tax burdens of those who could more readily increase compensation to cover income tax burdens, these being the highly skilled workers, the executives, professionals, and business sole proprietors. Finally, increases in the pay of less skilled workers would reach the point where their compensation would exceed the value of their contribution to production, so much so as to risk their jobs, particularly if these workers could be replaced by more mechanized means of production. And when this actually happened, the loss of jobs was blamed upon automation, and America was confronted with the phenomenon of a vast number of "poor people," despite the continuance of what was referred to as an "unparalleled prosperity."

The labor unions operated to assist the unskilled workers in keeping wages on a pattern that compensated for price increases, but the unions did next to nothing by way of attempting to stop the nonproductive Government spending that was the basic cause of the spiraling prices. The futility of the wage-increase approach can best be demonstrated with dollar-and-cents figures by considering the case of a hypothetical worker whose wages over a twenty-year period had moved upward under the so-called wage-price spiral to increase from $3,420.03 in 1943 to $6,878.92 in 1962. Although the wages of this hypothetical worker had doubled, he had to contribute to Federal income tax collections directly through tax payments (or withholding) and, of course, he also had to bear the tax burdens of others indirectly by paying higher prices for the things he bought. How the hypothetical worker has fared during twenty years of allegedly unparalleled American prosperity is shown in Table 17.

In reviewing the figures in Table 17 one might conclude that the worker was at least able to maintain the same purchasing power in spite of increased taxes and prices. However, such a conclusion would be only half right, because a status quo purchasing power would not provide for the expansion of American household budgets that had occurred between the years 1943 and 1962. Bear in mind that in 1943 rationing was in effect, and new automobiles and many

67

TABLE 17

HOW A WORKER'S STANDARD OF LIVING
HAS DECREASED DESPITE A DOUBLING OF WAGES

	Gross Earnings	Federal F.I.C.A. and Income Taxes Withheld	Take-Home Pay Actual	In 1943 Dollars*
1943	$3,420.03	$ 229.67	$3,190.36	$3,190.36
1962	6,878.92	1,412.10	5,466.82	3,127.02

Total F.I.C.A. and Federal income taxes
withheld, 1943–1962: $16,361.42

Source: Computed upon the basis of earnings stated.

*The basis of conversion is the Consumer Price Index published by the Bureau of Labor Statistics.

other items could not even be purchased. Contrariwise, in 1962 the worker could buy whatever he could afford, and by then many new products developed since 1943 could have been purchased, citing television as an example. Finally, one should acknowledge, too, that even the Consumer Price Index does not fully measure price increases, such as the cheapening of quality that is a price increase in disguise.

How could the American worker expand his budget, even though income taxes and price increases were at least freezing his purchasing power at World War II levels? One method was to have the worker's wife join him in working to help support the family. And here is the proof that this has happened:

TABLE 18

	Female Labor Force 1940	1970
Single Females Employed	6,710,000	6,965,000
Married Females Employed	5,040,000	19,799,000

Source: U. S. Department of Commerce.

The second method was for the worker to borrow as never before. And most American workers adopted both methods.

One might wonder how American workers and their wives would have reacted to the explanation that the wife had to work to help support government employees who were contributing nothing to production. This explanation would not constitute an exaggeration, since the increased taxes and higher prices that prompted the wife to work were the direct result of having millions of Government workers supported by the economy, without these workers contributing anything to the production of goods and services needed and wanted by the consuming public.

Those with an understanding of tax history could seek to argue that the plight of the American worker was nothing new. They could contend that since the dawn of civilization the ordinary worker and the consumer have always borne the brunt of any nation's tax burden. But such argument would fail to acknowledge that the Federal income tax, as perverted from its original intent, had introduced two factors not ordinarily associated with the process of consumers bearing a nation's tax burden. These factors were (1) an excessively high cost of tax administration and collection, and (2) an extremely high additional cost that flowed from tax-avoidance procedures. The additional tax administration and the tax-avoidance cost have had to be included in the prices paid by the consumer, together with the cost of the taxes actually collected by the Government.

It is not difficult to prove that the consumer's prices must of necessity include the costs of a wasteful tax procedure. Turning first to the matter of the cost of tax administration and collection, it should be borne in mind that a transaction or receipts tax would be simple and easy to administer, so that the cost of administering and collecting such tax would be relatively low when related to the amount of taxes collected. This is so because there cannot be much question or dispute as to the dollars to be reported as transactions or receipts. However, the same situation does not apply with respect to the income tax, because the matter of taxable income is the subject of much conjecture and uncertainty. The Internal Revenue Code defines the income that is taxable and explains how it is to be taxed, and the Code consists of hundreds of pages of single-spaced legal text. This has had to be explained in turn by hundreds of regulations and rulings, and the conglomerate mess has invited massive litigation involving many thousands of court decisions. These conditions could only have resulted in a high cost of income tax administration that has had to be loaded into the prices the consumer pays along with the taxes.*

Considering next the matter of the cost of income tax avoidance, the income tax has encouraged the process of either earning low-taxed or no-tax income, or of increasing deductible expenses against high-taxed income so as to reduce the annual taxable income and the tax. In fact, the high rates of the income tax have caused taxpayers to prefer whatever benefits could be obtained by them out of deductible expenses instead of being satisfied with the pennies that would remain after the application of confiscatory rates to larger amounts of income obtained out of a more economical business conduct. That tax avoidance has been extremely popular has been demonstrated by the absence of cost-saving techniques in business operations in any area where the business (or the management) could benefit from otherwise unnecessary expenditures, such as luxurious offices, expensive business travel and entertainment, and the complete lack of economy in advertising, promotion and research activities. These have all reflected the decision of taxpayers generally that it is better to enjoy whatever can be salvaged out of these wasteful procedures than to struggle to increase taxable income, out of which little could be salvaged after paying high taxes. These wasteful procedures have increased the costs of business operation so as to increase, too, the prices the consumer has had to pay.

Business executives and those in the professions have had an alternative to the tax-deductible-expense gimmick. These persons have

*The American Bar Foundation has estimated that taxpayers' efforts in filling out income tax returns for 1967 were worth about 1.3 billion dollars. The Commissioner of Internal Revenue's Annual Report for the June 30, 1968 fiscal year reveals Internal Revenue salaries for that year were 0.7 billion dollars. This totals 2 billion dollars, but even this huge sum does not include the costs of thousands of accountants, attorneys, Federal Judges, and clerks that are in one way or another involved in the administration of the income tax. Nor does it include any costs for record keeping, printing, forms, etc., all of which costs have become imbedded in the prices the consumer has had to pay.

70

been in a position of writing their own ticket as to compensation or fees, because their services have been very much in demand. And their demands have literally shoved executive compensation and professional fees through the roof in the wild scramble to produce an income that, if fully taxed, would yield some spending money. There has been little resistance to these demands for compensation or fees, because the payments have been tax deductible. And quite a number of executives have tired of this futile struggle to increase fully taxed income so as to yield small amounts of after-taxes income. These executives have demanded (and have been granted) various untaxed fringe benefit arrangements, even though the cost of these had to be added to the prices charged the consumer. Yes, the consumer has paid and paid.

So I conclude that the American consumer has had to pay the nation's income taxes, the costs of collecting the taxes, and even the costs of resisting and avoiding the income taxes. But there is even something more to the tragedy of how the income tax has shoved the consumer's prices ever upwards. The American consumer has also had to pay the cost of raising capital for American business. Weird as this statement may appear to be, it happens to state a fact, even though it will require some detailed explanation to enable one to understand this fact fully.

I shall start the explanation by stating that ordinarily business corporations have provided their capital out of funds obtained from their shareholders, i.e., they have raised capital through sale of shares. Of course, this capital has always been supplemented to some extent with borrowed funds. However, corporate managements are not ordinarily inclined to overborrow, because this has involved an interest cost, not to mention the problem of being able to pay the debts when they are due for payment. But the high-rate income tax has changed these traditional concepts for raising corporate capital on a sound basis.

Stating the case squarely, interest on debt has been tax deductible, whereas dividends paid to shareholders could not be deducted. Yet the money coming either from borrowing or from shareholders is equally usable as corporate capital. Hence, every incentive has been

71

provided to borrow instead of to obtain capital from shareholders through the sale of shares. And corporations have borrowed and borrowed, and the interest they have paid on these borrowings has become part of their costs and has become imbedded in the prices the consumer has had to pay.

Some technically minded folk might seek to dispute the foregoing comments that describe how prices have been kited by the income tax. These persons might insist that prices charged consumers have depended upon competitive conditions. That conclusion is completely valid. However, since most of the business firms in practically every type of business or industrial pursuit have followed the identical route of indulging in tax-induced spending and borrowing, most competitors in any business have established prices on the basis of cost factors that are identically loaded with the unnecessary costs and the interest expense that have been dictated entirely by income tax considerations. Incidentally, in a business atmosphere such as has prevailed for the past two decades, competition has in many instances been *de minimis*. Hence, the highest-cost producers (having the most tax-deductible expense and the largest amounts of tax-deductible interest) have found that their competitors have been only too willing to follow the high prices posted by the higher-cost producers. And the overborrowed status of business corporations can only contribute to the belief that the American consumers have been paying some needlessly high prices to enable business to pay the interest on these borrowings. One could include the observation that tax-inspired borrowing has been the culprit most responsible for the national tight-money dilemma.

A national sales tax could not have corrupted the price structure and the national economy as has the income tax. Moreover, a sales tax would be more economical to administer and to collect. And sales tax collections would have had to be turned over to the government without much controversy or litigation. These tax collections by business could not have been used for any other purpose in the manner that the portion of prices intended to pay the income tax has been

72

used. Whenever the rate of sales tax would have been increased or decreased, the taxpayer would have known about that, too. Unfortunately, most taxpayers dislike a sales tax, because when a taxpayer pays that form of tax he knows full well that he is paying the tax.

This completes the process of explaining how the changes in the income tax law provided the Federal Government with the power to inflate the economy—to cause the amount of money and credit to exceed available goods and services, the condition that is inflation. But a perfectly logical question remains to be answered: When will this income-tax-inspired inflation end?

There are two alternative answers to that question, and these are (1) inflation will end provided the income tax can be abolished and replaced with a less inflationary tax, or (2) inflation will end once America has become completely pauperized: when the government has taken all property for the purpose of continuing its own nonproductive pursuits.

No doubt the second answer is apt to be refuted by the reader, since the reader believes that the income tax can tax only income. Any beliefs of the reader notwithstanding, the second answer is supported by no less an authority than a decision of the United States Supreme Court. As a matter of fact, that decision, though it may have received little publicity, was actually issued by the Supreme Court more than 35 years ago. And as an attorney with considerable experience in tax matters, I feel called upon to note that it is not unusual for the Federal Government to exhume old court decisions whenever these are needed to justify a change regarding income tax matters.

What the Supreme Court said in 1934 is that the Federal income tax is not restricted to the taxing of net income, because the Court concluded that Congress has the power to decide what deductions are to be allowed in reaching the income subject to tax.* The Supreme Court expressed it this way:

*New Colonial Ice Co., Inc. v. Helvering, 292 U.S. 435, 13 A.F.T.R. 1180.

The power to tax income like that of a new corporation is plain and extends to the gross income. Whether and to what extent deductions shall be allowed depends upon legislative grace; and only as there is clear provision therefor can any particular deduction be allowed.

The conclusion of the Supreme Court as expressed in the language quoted should leave little doubt that gross income could also mean gross receipts. The Supreme Court had really decided that except for the fact that Congress had exercised its legislative grace by providing that costs and expenses could be deducted in arriving at the income subject to tax, *the income tax law would have taxed gross receipts.* Hence, the Supreme Court was really saying that the Sixteenth Amendment had given Congress the power to enact a sales (gross income or gross receipts) tax, but Congress had been generous (through the exercise of its legislative grace) so as to have the income tax apply only to net income, i.e., income computed after the deduction of costs and expense. Imagine the effect of applying high income tax rates to gross receipts, which is just another name that could be applied to sales!

As a matter of fact, the United States Supreme Court reiterated its view that the Federal income tax could be employed by Congress to tax receipts without allowing any deductions, should Congress so decide. This later decision was issued by the Court four years later, in 1938. In the intervening period the United States Court of Appeals for the Second Court had issued a decision that "toned down" the views previously expressed by the Supreme Court.* Nevertheless, the second time around the Supreme Court merely reiterated its previously stated view,** and said:

> Moreover, every deduction from gross income is allowed as a matter of legislative grace, and "only as there is clear provision therefor can any particular deduction be allowed . . . A taxpayer seeking a deduction must be able to point to an applicable statute and show that he comes within its terms." *New Colonial Ice Co.* v. *Helvering,* 292 U.S. 435, 440, 54 S. Ct. 788, 790, 78 L. Ed. 1348.

Davis v. United States, 87 Fed. 2d 323.
**In *White et al.* v. *United States,* 305 U.S. 281.

74

Hence, the U. S. Supreme Court has made available to Congress a legal route for amending the income tax law so as to exclude *all deductions* from income, and thereafter to tax gross receipts. This should leave little doubt that there is an unlimited reservoir of funds, dipping eventually into all privately owned property, with which the Federal Government can continue the inflation of the economy as described in this chapter.

The conclusion is plain. Except for the remote possibility of Americans abolishing the Federal income tax, inflation will continue until there remains nothing left to be subject to the income tax. Perhaps the reader has been shocked by the suggestion contained in this chapter that the government could seize privately owned property to continue its inflationary spending. But the reader should note that some government officials have already assumed that privately owned property belongs to the government. This assumption exists in the contention of these officials that the Government does not need gold to back up foreign-held dollars, since America has untold wealth in forms other than gold. Hence, these Government officials are already failing to distinguish between the gold the Government owns, and the untold wealth owned by private American citizens.

Of course, the Government officials may now explain that they have mentioned the "untold wealth" merely as the source for continued income tax collections that could provide funds somehow to satisfy the foreign holders of American dollars. However, since annual income tax collections are already insufficient to finance the annual inflationary spending by the Government, the officials would be drawing a distinction without a difference.

CHAPTER 5

The Government's Power
to Inflate in Operation
(World War II and Thereafter)

The outbreak of World War II in September 1939 came at a time when America was still trying to get over the effects of an economic slide that was nearing its tenth anniversary. At that time unemployment remained at high levels and the nation's productive plants had been allowed to deteriorate. During the ten long years of depression the operation of business under restrictive Federal laws had provided very little incentive to maintain productive capacity at the levels that had existed at the close of the New Era boom.

In one respect, however, America had experienced a most substantial expansion. This was in the size of the Federal Government bureaucracy. Further, and as was explained in Chapter 4, the Federal Government had developed a method for obtaining funds to inflate the economy through the changes in the income tax law that gave it the power to tax the earnings of the workers.

About the time that the war started, this massive government bureaucracy was hard pressed to find something to control, so as to justify its size. And the government's latent power to tax and to spend had been exercised at a slow pace because of depression conditions. However, the outbreak of war brought both the operation of the bureaucracy, and the taxing and spending power, up to full force. In many respects, the change-over to war conditions required those in government to pull a "quick switch," and they did just that.

Practically instantaneously, those in government forgot about their claim that productive capacity had been overbuilt, and they promptly offered tax incentives to manufacturers to encourage them to expand their plants. Any industrialist who might have balked at increasing plant capacity that had been proclaimed as overbuilt only a few months earlier was encouraged nevertheless to build a plant addition, because the entire cost of the addition could be charged against heavily taxed income over a period of no more than five years. And this war-production effort got started before America had even entered the war as a direct participant.

The building of new plants as defense facilities, coupled with lend-lease production activity and followed later with the war production, was able to cause a relatively prompt turnabout in the American economy. Idle plants were reactivated. And even as idle plants were pressed into service and made larger, so American manpower was brought back into full activity. Skilled persons who had either been unemployed or had been working at practically any job during the depression were able to resume the work for which they had been trained and for which they had experience. Somewhat as in the case of the American productive plant that had once been considered "overbuilt," the depression surplus of persons with the required skills for industrial production soon vanished. And since the younger men were being drafted for service in the Armed Forces, the possibility of training additional skilled manpower was remote. This is where "Rosie the Riveter" entered the American factory arena. Rosie was representative of the solution devised to meet the problem of the skilled-worker shortage. The solution was to provide minimal training to large numbers of persons to enable each of them to perform a small fragment of a factory operation, and these persons did contribute to overall industrial output.

The Federal Government had to perform another quick switch when it came to the food supply. During the depression those in government had urged a reduction in food production, but after the war started food immediately proved to be in short supply. So the Federal Government invoked food rationing. And in late 1942, price, wage and salary freezing were added to the war-induced restraints upon the economy.

Hence during the relatively short space of time between late 1939 and late 1942, the American economy had become reactivated. Plant facilities and human resources were applied to the work function that they had been waiting to perform during the long depression that had lasted from 1930 to 1939. Of course, the end result of war production was an entirely new development. The war demands for productive manpower, coupled with the manpower needs of the Armed Forces, most perceptibly changed the totals of the employed and the unemployed:

TABLE 19

EFFECT OF WORLD WAR II UPON EMPLOYMENT

Year	Persons in the Armed Forces	Persons in the Civilian Labor Force	Persons Unemployed
	(millions of persons)		
1939	0.37	45.75	9.48
1940	0.54	47.52	8.12
1941	1.62	50.35	5.56
1942	3.97	53.75	2.66
1943	9.02	54.47	1.07
1944	11.41	53.96	0.67
1945	11.44	52.82	1.04

Source: Bureau of Labor Statistics.

And the recently developed skills of the Federal Government in collecting taxes and in spending money were promptly converted to the financing of a war economy. It did not require much time for Federal Government spending to surpass the large sums that had been expended during the depression. As with war production, the spending had started even before America officially became a war participant (Table 20).

Nevertheless, in spite of a very active war economy, quite a number of Americans refused to depart from the conservative practices

TABLE 20

COMPARISON OF FEDERAL EXPENDITURES—
DEPRESSION ERA vs. WORLD WAR II PERIOD
TOTAL FEDERAL BUDGET EXPENDITURES
(in billions of dollars)

| Depression Era | | World War II Period | |
Year	Federal Expenditures	Year	Federal Expenditures
1932	4.66	1940	9.06
1933	4.60	1941	13.26
1934	6.65	1942	34.04
1935	6.50	1943	79.37
1936	8.42	1944	94.99
1937	7.73	1945	98.30
1938	6.77	1946	60.33
1939	8.84		

Source: Bureau of the Budget.

developed during the Great Depression. Many business and financial leaders remembered too well how those in government had only a couple of years earlier expressed criticism that the leaders of American industry had overbuilt the economy during the 1920s. Hence even many of the industrialists engaged in heavy war production continued to keep their fingers crossed. A number of these expressed the view that production plants would be "a dime a dozen" after the war.

Meanwhile, members of the consuming public patiently suffered the indignities of poor quality products and sloppy services by consoling themselves that things would be different after the war. And their memories of depression experiences, coupled with the short supply of consumer goods, combined to keep consumer spending at relatively low levels during the war. Obviously, the disinclination to spend contributed toward the payment of debts, many of which had remained unpaid since the boom period of the 1920s. And those who had no old debts to pay simply saved their money. Of course, this universal dedication to saving could be said to have been "forced" in great part, since consumer goods were not generally available for purchase and the goods that

were available were not of a quality that would inspire much inclination to purchase.

The general attitude displayed during the war of looking upon the
active war economy as merely a sort of breathing spell during a
depression was best evidenced by a disinterest in stock speculation.
Although corporate profits had increased perceptibly, and the financial condition of many corporations had improved, the Dow Jones
Industrial Stock Average had hardly acknowledged this betterment
in conditions. In fact, immediately after the close of World War II,
the high in that Average was at the same level as its 1937 high, the
latter having been set just before President Roosevelt's public out-
burst against high prices in April of 1937. The following tabulation
reveals how this Stock Average had fluctuated:

TABLE 21

ANNUAL HIGHS AND LOWS
OF
DOW JONES INDUSTRIAL STOCK AVERAGE

Year	Annual High	Date	Annual Low	Date
1937	194.40	March 10	113.64	Nov. 24
1938	158.41	Nov. 12	98.95	March 31
1939	155.92	Sept. 12	121.44	April 9
1940	152.80	Jan. 3	111.84	June 10
1941	133.59	Jan. 10	106.34	Dec. 23
1942	119.71	Dec. 26	92.92	April 28
1943	145.82	July 14	119.26	Jan. 8
1944	152.53	Dec. 16	134.22	Feb. 7
1945	195.82	Dec. 11	157.35	Jan. 24

Source: Taken from table in *Barron's Weekly*

V.J. Day signaled the end of World War II and all America was
happy. But the greatly expanded Federal bureaucracy was in somewhat of a dilemma. During the depression the government had an
excuse for tinkering with the economy, and during the war those in
government needed no excuse—the war gave them the authority to
act. What was to happen now that the war was over? How could the
members of the Federal bureaucracy continue to insist that they
were indispensable for the presumed management of an economy

80

that was neither mired in a depression nor beset with war-production problems?

In fact, quite a number of thinking Americans had expected to
experience an immediate postwar slump, after which they expected
the economy to stabilize, but without the economy returning to
depression depths. This was the maximum extent of their optimism.
These persons recognized that most of the conditions that had kept
the economy depressed during the long interval of 1930 to 1939 had
disappeared by 1945 only by force of the financial improvement of
business firms and personal budgets during the war. Nevertheless,
they anticipated that this financial improvement could hold the
economy above depression levels.

But the erstwhile economic planners in the Federal bureaucracy
were even less optimistic. They expected that the return of millions
of G.I.'s to civilian life would push the unemployment rolls back up
into the millions. Some persons in government even went so far as
to suggest that it might be economically feasible to keep the G.I.'s in
the Armed Forces for a time after the war was over, and until the
G.I.'s could be absorbed into the civilian work force. But the great
bulk of Americans had had enough of war, and they were ready to
face up to the problems of a reconversion of the economy to peacetime pursuits.

Contrary to what generally had been expected to happen, a postwar slump did not take place. And there were all kinds of reasons
why there was no slump. The nation's productive capacity was no
longer overbuilt in relation to the potential postwar purchasing
power that had been considerably expanded through an accumulation of wartime savings. And there were homes to build, and to
repair, to repaint and to reroof. There were wardrobes to be replen-
ished. Automobiles, that had not been manufactured for several
years, were in great demand. And in the course of war production
many new products had been developed for which there should be
a peacetime application. So America got to work.

The most significant economic change that had taken place during
the war was evidenced in the fact that at the close of World War II
Americans were no longer overburdened with private debt and

were no longer short of cash. During the war period debt had been reduced and cash had been accumulated. And there was an ample supply, too, of the equivalent of cash—U.S. Government Bonds. In technical terminology, at the close of 1945 America was in a high state of liquidity. As an example, the total deposits in all commercial banks of the nation had multiplied almost four times between 1932 and 1945, but the total loans of these same commercial banks had just about remained at the relatively depressed 1932 levels. And during this period all commercial banks, as a group, had been able to increase their cash and U.S. Government bondholdings by more than 100 billion dollars. Here are the complete statistics:

TABLE 22

BANK LIQUIDITY AT SELECTED YEARS
ALL COMMERCIAL BANKS IN THE UNITED STATES

Year	Total Deposits	Total Cash & U.S. Govt. Bonds	Total Loans	Ratio to Deposits	
				Total Cash & U.S. Govt. Bonds	Total Loans
		(in billions of dollars)			
1929	49.385	13.876	36.114	28.2%	72.1%
1932	35.658	13.220	22.001	37.1%	61.6%
1939	53.894	35.592	16.411	66.1%	30.6%
1945	136.727	114.293	23.697	84.0%	17.4%

Source: Federal Deposit Insurance Corporation records.

Really, the only fly in the ointment at the close of the war was the oversized Federal bureaucracy. The members of this were logical candidates for unemployment. However, the termination of the war did not cause the Bureaucracy to reduce its size as should have been expected. Nor were Federal income tax burdens reduced after the war as should also have been expected.* And in the preceding chapter it has been demonstrated how the continuation of the low annual tax exemption and the high tax rates after the war immediately kited wages and prices after price and wage freezing were terminated. In that chapter it was explained, too, that this was how the income tax

*However, promptly after the termination of the war the excess profits taxes assessed against corporations had been eliminated.

burden had been "passed on" to the American consumer to become a part of the price structure.

One can only conclude that the members of the Federal bureaucracy and the politicians knew that they had a good thing going in the income tax, and they were not about to perform what was logical or what was to be expected. And the Federal Government continued to tax and to spend. As a matter of fact, anyone scanning the tables of annual income tax collections would find it difficult to pinpoint the years in which war expenditures had been the cause of the extraordinary-sized income tax collections. The income tax collection figures attest to the fact that the Federal Government was determined to maintain the same level of income tax take, war or no war:

TABLE 23

FEDERAL INCOME TAX COLLECTIONS,
WORLD WAR II AND THEREAFTER
(in billions of dollars)

	Individuals	Corporations
1942	3.26	5.03
1943	6.63	10.00
1944	18.26	15.15
1945	19.03	16.40
1946	18.71	12.91
1947	19.69	9.68
1948	21.00	10.18
1949	17.93	11.56

Source: U.S. Treasury Department.

Hence, the Federal Government retained its power to inflate the economy.

Now, of course, the continued flow of income taxes into the Federal Treasury after the close of the war could have been applied to pay up the heavy Federal Government debt that had accumulated to such a huge sum during the war. This approach, too, would have reduced the power in the Government to inflate the economy. But the income tax collections were not used for that worthwhile purpose to any appreciable extent, even though the Federal debt was slightly reduced (Table 24).

TABLE 24

POST-WORLD WAR II
REDUCTION IN FEDERAL GOVERNMENT DEBT
(in billions of dollars)

Years		Years	
1945	258.7	1948	252.3
1946	269.4	1949	252.8
1947	258.3		

Source: Bureau of the Budget.

Instead of either reducing income taxes or using the huge tax collections to pay off the Federal debt, the Federal bureaucracy decided to continue in operation and on an expanded basis. All that was required to accomplish this objective was to find new and different ways for spending huge quantities of income tax dollars. The politicians in control of the Federal Government readily cooperated with this decision by enacting one new law after another, and one executive order after another, so as to extend the operations of the Federal bureaucracy into new fields. And, it need not be mentioned, there was no longer the excuse of a war emergency to justify Federal Government spending. Table 25 clearly demonstrates this.

In its zeal to spend tax dollars the Federal Government encouraged state and local governments to spend too. All kinds of programs were devised under which the Federal Government would pay a major portion of the cost of a state or local project. It would not be difficult to point to one instance after another where a local Chamber of Commerce, or a group of local business leaders, have held mass gatherings at which the growth of the Federal Government was decried with a collective smiting of the breasts. But having expressed such lofty philosophies, these opponents of Federal spending have found no factor of inconsistency in their rushing to Washington periodically to plead for a "Federal handout" for some local project. The prospect of Federal aid caused state and local governments to spend more than they received as taxes and charges. Despite the Federal aid, the total state and local debt increased (Table 26).

This increased spending by state and local governments had to be

TABLE 25

FEDERAL GOVERNMENT EXPENDITURES
(in billions of dollars)

Years	Expenditures	Years	Expenditures
1942	34.04	1956	66.22
1943	79.37	1957	68.97
1944	94.99	1958	71.37
1945	98.30	1959	80.34
1946	60.33	1960	76.54
1947	38.92	1961	81.52
1948	32.96	1962	87.79
1949	39.47	1963	92.64
1950	39.54	1964	97.68
1951	43.97	1965	96.51
1952	65.30	1966	106.98
1953	74.12	1967	126.73 (est.)
1954	67.54	1968	135.03 (est.)
1955	64.39		

Source: Bureau of the Budget.

TABLE 26

SPENDING BY STATE AND LOCAL GOVERNMENTS

	1950	1969
	(in billions of dollars)	
Total state and local government expenditures (excluding payments on debt)	27.9	131.6
Total state and local tax receipts and charges (excluding Federal aid)	23.2	113.0
Excess of expenditures over receipts	4.7	18.6
Federal Government aid	2.5	19.2
Total outstanding state and local debt at the end of the year	21.7	132.4

Source: U.S. Department of Commerce statistics.

paid for in the form of taxes by state and local taxpayers. Eventually these taxes would have to include, too, the payment of the huge bond issues that are nothing but an accumulation of deferred taxes remaining for payment in the future. Obviously, the increased state and local tax burden had to be heaped on the shoulders of the consumer in one way or another, even though the consumer had already been overloaded with the crushing burden of the Federal income tax and the costs related thereto.

The Federal bureaucracy stood to benefit enormously by extending spending to the financing of state and local projects. This gave the Federal Government a monopoly power, since it eliminated the possibility of there being any competition between the Federal Government and the state and local governments.* As a monopoly, the Federal Government could do what it pleased. Imagine the scope of power of a Federal Government that could seize income through the income tax, and then spend the tax collections through a network of state and local satellite governments located in every community in the land.

With the speed of lightning, this monopoly obtained control over all public and quasi-public projects. Educational institutions were expanded many times over. Concert halls, museums, art galleries and theatres were built. And every conceivable form of artistic appreciation was furnished with a palatial headquarters. Billions of dollars were expended in the building of expressways, superhighways and parking structures. Any conceivable project that could be dignified with the name "research" was provided with the funds needed for the activity. Never, except perhaps at the time of the building of the Pyramids of Egypt, had there occurred the expenditure of money and manpower representing so great a proportion of national wealth on projects that had little or no connection with the more mundane purpose of supplying products and services to satisfy man's daily living needs.

This massive spending did, of course, increase purchasing power. The spending also furnished more jobs. However, neither the spending nor the employment the spending financed contributed toward increasing the supply of goods and services the consumer needed and wanted to buy. And what seemed to escape notice was the cold fact that this spending and expansion of public projects actually

*The latest gimmick is for the Federal Government to share its tax receipts with state and local governments so as to increase the power and control in Washington.

thwarted the production of consumer goods and services. Even more important to the consumer, the cost of this spending increased the costs of business, and the increases in business costs, in turn, resulted in increased prices. To the extent that this spending for public projects had increased living costs (consumer budgets) independently of the price increases, there had to be renewed demands for higher compensation, which again had to push costs and prices upward in a vicious cycle. It could be said that inflation was fed by a powerhouse.

The validity of these conclusions concerning the effect upon the American consumer of this orgy of public-project expansion is easy to support merely by commenting upon the manner in which some of this expansion has been conducted. Practically all of the expansion in public and educational facilities has been accomplished by using high-priced urban land. This land bore a high price solely because it had a commercial utility; that is, it could produce high income when used for commercial purposes. However, when this land was converted to a public use, the land lost its economic utility since the land no longer produced income. At least, the land no longer served as the basis for high property-tax collections. And when large areas of high-cost urban land had been seized for expressway purposes, and otherwise usable structures had been demolished, the earnings of and the property-tax revenues from this land and the improvements were promptly lost forever.

Of course, the commercial ventures that formerly occupied these urban areas had to be relocated. But this involved a high cost of relocation. Further, this relocation could only be accomplished by moving commercial ventures into suburban and rural areas, and soon land became sufficiently scarce as to kite land prices in those areas. The relocation costs had to be borne by someone; and in the case of business firms the extra cost was soon reflected in higher prices. Sometimes the moving of a business out of an urban area convenient to customers and other business ventures required higher transportation costs in the continued conduct of the business thereafter, and these costs, too, had to be reflected in higher prices.

However, the relocation burden hit hardest those who had to

move their residence because of the wholesale preemption of land for public and quasi-public purposes. Oftentimes these people could not afford to move to more expensive locations. And, of course, these people could not increase their incomes to meet their increased budget costs in the way that a relocated business firm could recover relocation costs by increasing prices.

Another tragic result concerned the manner in which the relocation procedure, together with the building of expressways, wrecked the possibility of the survival of interurban and mass transit systems. Such systems lost customer patronage simultaneously with a perceptible increase in their costs of operation.

The Federal spending acted like a palliative that temporarily abated each facet of an economic illness only to cause another, more serious, malady. Concurrently, a public whose responsibility had been usurped by the government became apathetic and irresponsible while national problems were accumulating to massive proportions.

CHAPTER 6

The Kennedy Administration: Placing the Economy in a Boom-Bust Orbit

During the long period of time from the close of World War II until the year 1960, America experienced what was termed "creeping inflation." Federal spending had been keeping money and credit (the demand) continuously in excess of the available goods and services (the supply), but the crushing income tax burden restricted spending by consumers and by those in business.

However, in 1961 the Kennedy Administration set in motion the greatest boom-bust pattern in American history by a forced increase of consumer and business spending. Strange as it may seem, this has never been explained to the American public. The economic effect of President Kennedy's lighting a fuse to cause an explosion is a well-kept secret except for this action having been approved of by a British publication.*

*The Economist of May 10, 1969, published in London, contained an article entitled "Organization for Growth" which stated, "In January, 1961, President Kennedy therefore inherited an economy which had at any rate had all cost-push inflation squeezed temporarily out of its system . . ." This same article also stated, "By any reasonable measurement, the Democratic administrations from 1961 to 1969 gave the United States eight golden years of economic advance, with the greatest benefits going to the most poor."

It is interesting to note that President Kennedy (like President Roosevelt) expressed dissatisfaction about the state of the American economy when he took office. (And this was after almost thirty years of continued massive spending by the Government bureaucracy.) Upon his taking office, Kennedy said:

> In short, the American economy is in trouble. The most resourceful industrialized country on earth ranks among the last in economic growth. Since last spring our economic growth rate actually receded. Business investment is in a decline. Profits have fallen below predicted levels. Construction is off. A million unsold automobiles are in inventory. Fewer people are working—and the average work week has shrunk well below 40 hours. Yet prices have continued to rise—so that now too many Americans have less to spend for items that cost them more to buy.*

But even more interesting was the fact that President Kennedy did not follow President Roosevelt's lead in blaming the empty plants upon an overexpansion of productive facilities. Nor did President Kennedy claim that the million unsold automobiles were the result of any forced production of American industry. Instead, President Kennedy urged a greater expansion, i.e., a higher economic growth. Here was President Kennedy's solution for an economy in trouble:

> We cannot afford to waste idle hours and empty plants while awaiting the end of a recession. We must show the world what a free economy can do—to reduce unemployment, to put unused capacity to work, to spur new productivity, and to foster higher economic growth within a range of sound fiscal policies and relative price stability.*

It was difficult to understand how the late President Kennedy intended to foster additional economic growth for an economy that had become overloaded with heavy costs and increased prices through the economic growth thus far brought about by government spending. The simple truth was that the American people could no longer carry the burden of the cost of supporting literally millions of nonproducers employed in the various government programs that

*State of the Union message, January 30, 1961.

90

had spurred an alleged economic growth. The massive government spending had overloaded the people with high prices and high taxes.

But the solution for all this was simple; at least it was to President Kennedy and his advisors. You had to give the already over-stimulated economy the most massive dose of additional stimulant possible. In simpler terminology: it was his solution that a tax cut and an increased government-spending program be invoked at one and the same time. This is not the author's version of what happened; it was actually so described, and in a boastful manner, by the Council of Economic Advisers (better known as the C.E.A.). This is what the C.E.A. said:

> This tax cut was unprecedented in many respects. When fully effective in 1965, it added more than $11 billion to private purchasing power —the largest stimulative action ever undertaken in peacetime. It was enacted while the federal budget was in deficit and while expenditures were rising. It was designed explicitly to sustain and invigorate expansion up to potential output rather than to combat an existing or imminent recession. This major action was followed by the enactment of a phased reduction in excise taxes in the spring of 1965.

Before explaining how the Kennedy Administration propelled the American economy into a decisive boom-bust orbit, let us reemphasize that every worker's income taxes had been passed on to his employer in the form of increased compensation; the employer had in turn passed the increased payroll expense on to the consumer as higher prices and, of course, the employer had included his own income taxes in the bill. Hence, at the time that we are talking about, in the early 1960s, the inflated price structure included everyone's income taxes so that American consumers were bearing the crushing burden of bureaucratic extravagance at all levels of government in the high prices they were paying. In fact, this was the economic condition that had caused the economy to falter.

This meant, of course, that if the income tax were to be reduced, you also had somehow to reduce wages, prices and salaries, otherwise the tax reduction would simply create an extra flow of spending money. The danger in this was that any increase in spending would

91

increase the demand for goods and services, but without necessarily prompting a corresponding increase in the supply of goods. Hence, the danger could be interpreted as one of introducing the greatest inflation possible.

Nevertheless, income taxes were reduced without consideration of the rampant inflation that this would bring. The first tax reduction involved business firms, and in this instance the planners decided that business firms could take some of the tax dollars that they had collected from their customers and spend those dollars on machinery and equipment. Of course, this gimmick of diverting dollars that had been collected from the consumer as tax payments, and using these dollars instead to purchase equipment, had to be dignified somehow, and it was. It was labeled an "investment credit." (It should be emphasized that this was really a forgiveness of tax, and it was not the same as the customary depreciation deduction from income subject to tax.) For the approximate period that the "investment credit" was in existence, Internal Revenue Service reported, for fiscal years ended June 30th, the following reduction in tax revenues through the allowance of said credit, stated in billions of dollars:

1962	0.8	1965	1.7
1963	1.1	1966	2.0
1964	1.3	1967	2.1

American business firms had collected these billions of dollars from consumers to pay income taxes, but the billions were used instead to buy machinery and equipment, as is demonstrated by Table 27.

After having permitted American business to use the tax dollars furnished by customers to buy equipment, the Federal bureaucracy turned next to the income of taxpayers, both corporate and personal. Here again, the tax dollars that were being paid by the wage-and-salary worker were being obtained from the employer in the form of increased pay, and the employer in turn was passing his workers' tax burden plus his own on to the American consumer. Nevertheless, the bureaucrats decided upon a tax cut for both personal and corpo-

TABLE 27

PRIVATE PURCHASES OF PRODUCERS'
DURABLE EQUIPMENT
(billions of
dollars)

1961	28.7	1965	44.9
1962	32.5	1966	53.1
1963	34.9	1967	55.3
1964	39.8	1968	58.5

Source: Department of Commerce.

rate income taxpayers. And the only possible result was to furnish all taxpayers with extra spending money as the C.E.A. had boastfully stated.

This extra spending caused the American economy to take off like a time bomb. Those in business found their sales and income soaring, but they did not know what they had done to produce this "success." The fact of the matter was that they had done nothing. It was the action of the Federal Government that had caused the upsurge in the economy to new inflationary heights, by the simple process of permitting funds obtained by taxpayers to pay income taxes to be used for other spending purposes.

The "tax cuts" were applied in part in 1963, and with an additional reduction in rates in 1964. As increased spending money was provided through the tax cuts, prices moved upward, followed, of course, by wages and salaries. And the published statistics clearly demonstrated the wild economic binge that followed the tax cuts. For example, in the field of manufacturing, both employees and corporations shared in the tax-cut millennium (Table 28).

But the well-laid plans of the Federal establishment to revitalize the economy through the "investment credit" and the "tax cut" upset the grand plan of the Federalists to have the economy move ahead under the impulse of what they had theretofore described as "creeping inflation." This tinkering with the income tax had turned creeping inflation into a gallop. Perhaps this result was not recognized immediately; nevertheless it did not require much time for the

TABLE 28

THE KITING OF INCOMES
THROUGH INFLATING THE ECONOMY
WITH TAX REDUCTIONS

	Wages and Salaries Paid by Manufacturers	Manufacturing Corporations' Income After Income Taxes	Dividends Distributed by Manufacturing Corporations
	(in millions of dollars)		
1959	$ 95,776	$13,643	$ 5,945
1960	99,424	12,938	6,265
1961	99,718	11,913	6,086
1962	108,158	14,400	7,185
1963	112,888	15,144	7,574
1964	120,460	17,856	8,268
1965	130,067	20,662	9,278
1966	145,301	24,670	10,090
1967	152,265	22,275	10,215
1968	166,370	22,752	11,375
1969	180,112	19,739	11,256
1970	181,654	16,911	11,045

Source: Department of Commerce.

extra-heavy hypodermic to produce a boom-bust pattern through greatly increased spending.

The extra volume of spending far exceeded the funds supplied by the investment credit and the tax cut, because these "tax gimmicks" supplied only the down payment for the amounts spent. For example, when American business took advantage of the "credit" and purchased additional machinery and equipment, extra money was needed to pay that part of the cost of the equipment that was not supplied by the tax credit. And, since interest on borrowings was tax deductible, it was logical to assume that the money needed for tax-inspired equipment purchases would be borrowed. And it was borrowed. The tax cut increased nonbusiness borrowings, too, because, when taxpayers were given some extra spending money through the "tax cut," they followed the traditional American policy of expanding this extra spending money considerably through borrowing. Finally, since the Federal Government was losing tax revenues through the investment credit and the tax cut, the Federal Government borrowed, too.* State and local governments could not function in this atmosphere without joining in the spending, and they spent and they borrowed. And the debt of just about everyone hit new heights, as the following tabulation indicates:

TABLE 29

THE KITING OF DEBT THROUGH INFLATING
THE ECONOMY WITH TAX REDUCTIONS

	Federal Debt*	State and Local Debt*	Long-Term Private Corporation Debt*	Consumer Installment Credit**
	(In Billions of Dollars)			
1959	$245.1	$ 59.6	$129.3	$39.2
1960	243.3	64.9	139.1	42.8
1961	250.7	70.5	149.3	43.5
1962	258.9	77.0	161.2	48.0
1963	264.7	83.9	174.8	54.2
1964	271.5	90.4	192.5	60.5
1965	275.3	98.3	209.4	71.3
1966	283.0	104.8	231.3	77.5
1967	295.5	112.8	258.1	80.9
1968	313.3	123.2	286.1	89.9

*Source: Department of Commerce.
**Source: Federal Reserve.

The increased surge of national spending engendered by the investment credit and the tax cut increased the demand for goods and services without also prompting a comparable increase in the supply. And prices were shoved upwards because of the widened gulf between demand and supply. The Consumer Price Index clearly demonstrated that result (Table 30).

The tax cut brought about other changes in economic conditions that made the boom-bust pattern even more certain. For example, in the case of those with higher amounts of earnings, the appetite of these persons for additional increases in after-tax income became considerably whetted by the tax cut. It should be borne in mind that

*As the C.E.A. had stated, the Federal Government did not decrease its spending despite the fact that the investment credit and the tax cut would reduce government revenues.

TABLE 30

CONSUMER PRICE INDEX

1958	100.7	1965	109.9
1959	101.5	1966	113.1
1960	103.1	1967	116.3
1961	104.2	1968	121.2
1962	105.4	1969	127.7
1963	106.7	1970	133.6
1964	108.1		

Source: Bureau of Labor Statistics.

confiscatory tax rates applied to the higher brackets of income had discouraged such persons from asking for salary increases. However, the reduction of the high tax rates through the tax cut provided a larger after-tax income out of every salary increase. Similarly, those in professional activity were provided with an incentive to increase fees.

The following tabulation provides some ideas as to the extra spending money the tax cut provided for those in higher income brackets:

TABLE 31

TAX CUTS APPLIED TO THE
UPPER-INCOME BRACKETS

Income Bracket	1964 Income Tax Saving	1965 Income Tax Saving
$25,000.00 annual salary income*	$ 612.00	$ 978.00
$50,000.00 annual salary income*	1,829.00	2,684.00
$100,000.00 annual salary income*	4,808.00	7,116.00

Source: Computed as described.

*Assuming a married person with spouse and no dependents, no other income, and assuming also that the deductions represented 10 percent of income.

Hence, salaries that were already high were increased additionally, as were professional fees, because these persons were in a posi-

96

tion to demand, and get, increases.* All of these increases augmented costs, and this in turn propelled prices upward. And the consumers' burden became even more serious.

These newly developed sources of additional income for those with already large incomes spurred the buying of luxuries and the purchase of goods for the "man who has everything."

Since the tax cut had provided quite a number of persons with additional income beyond that needed for daily living, these persons could use that income to accumulate savings, or they could spend the additional income on luxuries. They did both. And the savings were used to buy stocks so they could capitalize on the completely obvious inflation and get additional low-taxed capital gain income.

Hence, it should have caused no surprise to find that shortly after the effects of the investment credit and the tax cut began to be felt, stock brokerage firms experienced a prosperity and a volume of business that caused their 1929 prosperity to pale into insignificance. The prosperity for the stock brokers was directly induced by funds released by the investment credit and the tax cuts. No matter what the Federal bureaucracy might have anticipated, these tax benefits were the direct cause for the renewed emphasis upon speculation.

For one thing, the "investment credit" plus the corporate tax cut served to increase the incomes of corporations. The increase in corporate incomes automatically made purchase of the shares of corporations more attractive, which whetted the appetites of potential stock buyers. The persons who were ordinarily inclined to purchase common stocks as investments now had increased funds (in the form of increased income after taxes) to invest.

That stock investment (or speculation) had increased perceptibly was clearly revealed by the figures published by the New York Stock Exchange on the annual volume of shares traded, in billions of dollars. Table 32 shows how the tax cut had caused the share-trading volume to soar upward:

*This is demonstrated by Internal Revenue statistics, because the total income of taxpayers in the 20-to-100-thousand-dollar bracket increased from 18.4 percent in 1960 to 25.3 percent as a percentage of total personal income reported to I.R.S. Even more dramatically, those reporting income of more than $100,000 accounted for only 5.4 percent of total personal income in 1960, but 9.2 percent in 1968.

TABLE 32

THE KITING OF NEW YORK STOCK EXCHANGE
SHARE-TRADING VOLUME BY INFLATING
THE ECONOMY WITH TAX CUTS

Year	Billions of Dollars of Shares Traded	Year	Billions of Dollars of Shares Traded
1962	47.341	1966	98.565
1963	54.887	1967	125.329
1964	60.424	1968	144.978
1965	73.200		

Source: New York Stock Exchange statistical sources.

This flurry of buying caused the Dow Jones Industrial Stock Average to move from 535.76 on June 26, 1962, to 995.15 on February 9, 1966.*

There should be little doubt but that the investment credit and the tax cut also contributed toward causing the United States balance-of-payments-deficit problem. The explanation starts with the reminder that these tax benefits had caused prices to skyrocket, and this of and by itself caused American prices to be out of line with the prices of competing foreign-made products. However, despite the price disadvantage that had flowed from the income tax tinkering of the Federal establishment, the Federal Government next proceeded to bring about tariff decreases. This could have had no other result than to spur considerably the importation of foreign goods. And one should even conclude that a large part of the spending money furnished Americans through the tax cut to invigorate the American economy ended up in the purchase of foreign-made goods. The statistics as to imports of foreign merchandise lend support to that conclusion (Table 33).

Hence we find that during a period in which exports of merchandise increased by 50 percent, imports almost doubled.

The Federal bureaucracy did not acknowledge the part it had played in fomenting a boom-bust pattern through the tax cut; but the

*The "Kennedy Tax Cuts" proved most rewarding to speculators, since net capital gain income reported by taxpayers zoomed from $5.3 billion in 1960 to almost $18 billion in 1968. These are Internal Revenue Service figures.

TABLE 33

THE KITING OF IMPORTS THROUGH
REDUCING TARIFFS AFTER INFLATING
THE ECONOMY WITH TAX CUTS

	Exports of Merchandise	Imports of Merchandise
	(in billions of dollars)	
1963	22.1	17.0
1964	25.3	18.6
1965	26.3	21.5
1966	29.4	25.5
1967	30.7	26.8
1968	33.6	33.0

Source: *Federal Reserve Bulletin.*

Federalists did the next best thing to coming clean with the American public. The bureaucracy recommended a surtax "to cool an overheated economy" as the next step; but there was no acknowledgment that the bureaucracy itself had furnished the heat.

Lest it be overlooked, it should be emphasized that the actions of the Federal Government in trying first to fire the economy with tax reductions, and thereafter attempting to cool off the spending conflagration with a surtax, most clearly demonstrate the power to inflate the economy that the government had obtained through the perversion of the Federal income tax, as was explained in depth in the preceding chapter. The scope of this power is so all-inclusive that it has even been exercised in extending financial assistance to a single taxpayer—a large corporation—in a situation that was actually "advertised" in the campaign literature of a United States Senator who was running for reelection.

The foregoing refers to the fact that Senator Gaylord Nelson (Wisconsin) apparently wanted recognition for the part he had played in the enactment of a tax bill intended to benefit one taxpayer. Senator Nelson's campaign literature contained a picture of workers entering a plant with the caption:

Workers enter the American Motors Corporation plant main gate at Kenosha. Helped by a $20 million tax write-off piloted through Congress by Nelson, American Motors now is in the black and competing hard with Detroit's Big Three—which, of course, means continued employment for thousands of Wisconsin families. Nelson and his colleague, William Proxmire, are regarded as one of the most effective teams in the U. S. Senate.

Senator Nelson's campaign advertisement should prompt a few questions. Had not the customers of American Motors really supplied the tax dollars that were later refunded to the Corporation? And when American Motors later went into "the black" were these specially designed tax refunds returned to the Federal Government? Was it not the American Motors shareholders, rather than the workers, that had really benefited from the special tax refunds? As a matter of fact, some time later, in October 1969, American Motors made an offer to purchase (acquire) another corporation, and the purchase offer included the proposition that American Motors would pay $10 million in cash.

But the reference to Senator Nelson's advertisement should not be restricted to the matter of how his efforts contributed to relieving the financial plight of one corporation. The income tax provision that had been amended through Senator Nelson's efforts specifically to benefit one corporation really presents a far more serious future hazard for all Americans. This observation refers to the fact that anyone conducting a business has the privilege of carrying back operating losses to years when there were profits, and to years in which taxes were paid, so as to recover the taxes paid in the earlier profitable years. This poses an intriguing question—what would happen should this particular income tax provision require large amounts of tax refunds to those in business, in the case of a national economic adversity customarily known as a depression? Stating the question simply —who would have to supply the funds needed to refund taxes to businesses claiming benefits under the loss carry-back provision?

The answer should be completely obvious. Only those who would continue to have salary or wage income that could be taxed during a depression, including those who would then continue to have income from a profitable business, could possibly pay the money

100

needed for these tax refunds. Taxpayers with income would have to increase their income tax payments so as to enable the government to operate, while at the same time expanding their tax payments to enable the government to make large refunds to businesses incurring operating losses. And those that would have income during a depression would also have to contribute at such time to the support of those who would be unemployed, because there is no similar "operating loss" provision for an unemployed worker. This is to say that if a worker loses his job, there is no way for him to get income tax refunds of the taxes he had paid while he was working and earning money.

When the antics of the Federal Government in using its power to inflate the economy are analyzed, as has been done in summary form in this chapter, the conclusion that emerges is quite frightening. That conclusion is that too great a proportion of this nation's financial resources have been expended upon activities that contribute next to nothing toward assuring the future support of the nation's people. It seems as if the Federal Government has reversed the procedure described in the biblical story of Joseph and Pharaoh Potifar. In that story, the reader will recall, under Joseph's God-inspired counsel Potifar stored up the excess crops of seven years of plenty so as to support his people during the seven years of famine that followed. Contrariwise, the Federal Government has expended the surplus of many years of plenty upon projects that cannot possibly contribute to the support of the people should a period of famine (depression) at any time occur in America's future.

Meanwhile, the American consumer has paid for the Government's inflating the economy by being forced to pay higher and higher prices. And when those consumers who were factory workers demanded exceedingly high wages with which to meet their kiting budgets, the Government blamed the consumer-workers for causing inflation! This is hard to believe, but it happens to be the truth.

The facts related in this chapter that demonstrate how Federal Government action directly caused the boom-bust economy of the later 1960s are startling. However, what is even more startling is the fact that an explanation of the explosion in prices resulting from this

101

tinkering with the economy has never been given to the American people, at least not to the author's knowledge. Typical of the public statements made by those in Government are the words expressed by Arthur Burns, Chairman of the U. S. Federal Reserve Board, who told an international gathering of bankers in Munich, West Germany, in June 1971:

> Our price performance has recently been better than that of many other industrial countries. This advantage is likely to continue and it should permit us to regain the competitive strength that we probably lost in the second half of the 1960s.*

Absent in these words is the suggestion that the American "competitive strength that we probably lost" was, in fact, unknowingly, but nevertheless deliberately, wrecked by the Federal Government through its use of the power to inflate the economy by means of the income tax.

*U.S. News & World Report, June 14, 1971.

CHAPTER 7

The Role of Nonprofit Organizations
in Inflating the Economy

The preceding chapter explained how the release of dollars intended for income tax payments had been diverted through the
investment credit and the tax cut to inflate the economy to boom-
bust proportions. It was explained, too, how this had caused an increase in buying of luxury goods and in speculation on the part of
those with substantial amounts of income. Meanwhile, however,
those in lower-income brackets found it difficult to meet their skyrocketing budget costs.

This contrast between the opulence experienced by some and the
budget difficulties that became the lot of others is further evidenced
by the changes that occurred on the matter of contributions to charities. Internal Revenue-published statistics clearly reveal a change
before and after these tax gimmicks had taken effect. The figures
reveal clearly that, comparing charitable contributions for 1968 with
those of 1962, there had occurred a substantial change in charitable
giving (Table 34).

Except for one assumption made by the author, this being the
modest estimate of a $20-per annum average contribution for each

TABLE 34

Income Bracket	Total Contributions in Billions of Dollars		Source of Data
	1962	1968	
Assumed estimated contributions of taxpayers that did not itemize their deductions (Estimate of $20.00 per taxpayer)*	$ .717	$ .826	Estimated
Contributions claimed as deductions on income tax returns of taxpayers with less than $5,000 of income	1.202	.831	Internal Revenue Statistics
Contributions claimed as deductions on tax returns of taxpayers having more than $5,000 but less than $10,000 of income	2.906	2.705	"
Contributions claimed as deductions on tax returns of taxpayers having more than $10,000 but less than $15,000 of income	1.270	2.662	"
Contributions claimed as deductions on tax returns of taxpayers having more than $15,000 of income	2.138	4.941	"
Total Individual Contributions	$8.233	$11.965	
Contributions by all United States corporations filing tax returns	$ .590	$ .830**	

*There were 35,839,490 such taxpayers in 1962, and 41,316,925 in 1968.

**Corporate contributions for 1967. More recent figures are not yet available.

taxpayer who did not itemize his contributions on tax returns filed, the tabulation sets forth the actual contributions claimed on tax returns according to Internal Revenue-published statistics.

Note how those taxpayers (itemizing deductions) with incomes of less than $10,000 contributed less to charities in 1968 than in 1962. However, between these same years taxpayers in the income bracket of between $10,000 and $15,000 doubled their contributions, and the contributions from those in the income bracket of more than $15,000 increased by more than 130 percent. Whether these results were

104

caused by changes in the number of persons in the income brackets, or changes in the pattern of the individuals making the contributions does not matter in noting the source of the spending. It is interesting to note, too, that U.S. corporations contribute a total to charities that is a modest fraction of the contributions by individuals, despite the publicity that is given an occasional large contribution by a corporation.

Even more noticeable in these contribution figures is the fact that the reported contributions of all personal income taxpayers increased by more than 45 percent between the years 1962 and 1968. And the total personal contributions of almost $12 billion for 1968 should attract attention for another reason. This figure represents an amount that exceeded the total annual output, in terms of net sales, of the entire steel-producing industry in the United States for 1968.

Am I suggesting that the steel-producing industry is more important than charity? I am, because that happens to be a fact. Except for the production of steel and other basic products, neither the workers of this nation nor those persons receiving charity could hope to survive. And this truism will be extended to say that you do not support the sick, the poor, the indigent and the aged with paper dollars, but with physical goods such as food, clothing and shelter, and other needs for human survival. It should require no extended argument to suggest that, unless the paper dollars contributed to charity can be exchanged and used to provide physical goods and services needed by those on charity, the contributing of money would be an exercise in futility.

But there is another "unless" that must be considered before the dollar figures of charitable contributions are considered as a reliable measurement of the actual relief provided for those needing and benefiting from charity. *Unless* the dollar contributions can provide the largest possible quantity of physical goods and services for those needing charity, the dollar contributions will not only fail to provide the charity needed, but will also serve to increase the number of persons that require charitable help. Should the latter condition prevail, charitable contributions would defeat, rather than assist, the conduct of valid charitable pursuits.

Why is this? The answer is really quite simple. Charitable activity, though most necessary, is nevertheless a parasitical pursuit from the standpoint of economical considerations, since the operation of charities contributes little, if anything, to the production of goods and services; yet goods and services form the basis for this operation. Hence, charitable activity and spending is completely similar to government activity and spending, the inflationary aspects of which were discussed in the preceding chapter. Both charity and government perform a needed service for the community, but as soon as this service is overexpanded, the economy suffers from an overload of money and credit in relation to the available goods and services, i.e., inflation. Obviously, inflation not only reduces the goods and services for charitable use that money contributions can provide, but also increases the number of people requiring charity.

Extending the consideration of the parasitical aspects of both government and charity, it should have been taken for granted that the perversion of the income tax that placed confiscatory tax rates on high incomes would ultimately release a flood of contributions at the peak of a "get rich quick" prosperity. This should have been expected, because high-income taxpayers had the choice of paying more dollars to the government as taxes, or increasing contributions to tax-deductible, nonprofit organizations. That this would spur human ingenuity to concoct all sorts of new forms of nonprofit enterprise, legally dedicated to advancing culture and science and education, could also have been taken for granted. One could note, too, that the individuals promoting big government and big nonprofit enterprise have the same characteristics. In fact, the leaders of these often switch from one operation to the other.

Obviously, the 45-percent increase in individual contributions between the years 1962 and 1968 amply supports the conclusion that the boom-bust pattern induced by the "investment credit" and the "tax cut" caused an upward surge in contributions. Further, the fact that the almost $12 billion in contributions for 1968 exceeded the output of a basic productive industry, the steel industry, revealed how purely parasitical and nonproductive enterprise was overwhelming productive enterprise.

106

We are now prepared for the explanation as to how a most decided expansion in nonprofit activity has substantially aided in inflating the economy so as actually to defeat the objective of providing charity. From this point forward the discussion shall concern "nonprofit activity" and "nonprofit organizations," because it would be practically impossible to gain acceptance of a critical analysis of any activity bearing the name "charity." This would be like expecting someone to accept an attack upon motherhood.

However, the foregoing is not an apology for the words that follow, because the label "charity" is no longer applicable to the many thousands of organizations that escape income taxation and that are privileged to accept tax-deductible contributions. Accordingly, the term "nonprofit organization" as hereafter used in this chapter will sometimes refer to such organizations as are ordinarily considered charitable (educational institutions, hospitals, churches, and organizations that support the needy), but will more often refer to the more recently conceived form of nonprofit activities. The latter will include all kinds of study and publication activities that qualify under the general description of being either scientific, literary or educational.

To provide the reader with an understanding as to the sheer size of nonprofit enterprise in terms of numbers, the reader's attention is directed to the fact that Internal Revenue's publication *Cumulative List of Organizations* lists all organizations to which tax-deductible contributions can be made. The December 31, 1966, edition consisted of 503 pages, with three columns of organizations in fine print on each page. Some of the pages include as many as 200 names per page. Unless Internal Revenue has totaled the number of organizations listed so as to present a reliable count, one can assume that something like 90,000 organizations were qualified to receive tax-deductible contributions on December 31, 1966. And two years later, as of December 31, 1968, the publication had been expanded to 596 pages!

One could start off with the suspicion that these many thousands of organizations cannot all be engaged in what is ordinarily considered charitable activity, such as supporting the poor, or helping the ill or the aged. This suspicion, should it motivate an examination of nonprofit activity, would reveal that many organizations are engaged in research, some of which is politically or semipolitically oriented. These organizations claim to advance the cause of education, and they flood the nation with books and booklets containing scholarly treatises on any subject conceivable. It is no exaggeration to suggest that if an executive or professional man should happen to be on the mailing list of several of these organizations, he will receive a quantity of "research publications" in one year that he could not possibly read, assuming, of course, that he had to devote at least some time to his business or to his profession.

This gargantuan network of tax-privileged, nonprofit organizations was not created because of a public need for their work. Instead, this mammoth activity is a direct result of the income tax changes as discussed in an earlier chapter. Stated in plain words, many taxpayers would rather contribute tax-deductible dollars to an organization that *might* do some good, rather than pay larger amounts of taxes to the government where the funds were apt to be wasted.

Actually, the sky is the limit when it comes to deductible contributions, since a tax-deductible contribution can be made to any organization that meets the following qualifications:

> organized and operated exclusively for religious, charitable, scientific, literary, or educational purposes or for the prevention of cruelty to children or animals

Who decides what is scientific, religious, or charitable, or what is literary, or what is educational? The answer may astonish you, but nevertheless the accurate answer is—those who organize and operate the scientific, the literary, or the educational enterprise. All one need do to set up an institution to which tax-deductible contributions can be made is to specify in the institution's charter one of the purposes listed above, and to use the contributions received for that purpose. And it does not matter much whether or not the operation of the institution may accomplish anything really scientific, or literary, or educational, so long as its activities, and its funds, are directed at *attempting to achieve* such end result.

Perhaps you refuse to accept my conclusions. No doubt you have been led to believe that Internal Revenue Service exercises a firm hand in deciding which organizations should continue to have the privilege of receiving tax-deductible contributions. But you should respect the fact that Internal Revenue Service is in no position to challenge the beliefs of an organization's founders and supporters that the organization does in fact accomplish any of the purposes specified in the tax law. Stated in the vernacular, "It is all a state of mind."

As a matter of fact, assuming that a nonprofit organization is organized for a religious, charitable, or other purpose as specified in the tax law, and seemingly operates to fulfill that purpose, there is no additional requirement that the organization accomplish anything constructive whatsoever. However, each tax-free nonprofit organization is specifically prohibited by the tax law from doing two things in the course of its operation.

The first of the prohibitions concerning operation is that:

No substantial part of the activities . . . is carrying on propaganda, or otherwise attempting, to influence legislation.

And the second of the prohibitions is that:

No part of the net earnings . . . inures to the benefit of any private shareholder or individual.

Hence, all that need be done to establish and to continue an institution that can be supported with tax-deductible contributions is (1) to choose some charitable, religious, scientific, literary or educational objective, (2) avoid any activities that involve propaganda or the influencing of legislation, and (3) make certain that the net earnings of the operation do not inure to the benefit of a private shareholder or individual.

At this point it should be stressed that the term "nonprofit" does not mean that a qualified organization under the tax law cannot have profits or earnings from operation. In fact, the law specifically acknowledges that these organizations could have profits when it states "no part of the *net earnings* . . . inures to the benefit of any private shareholder or individual." These conditions are stressed to clear up a generally held public belief that a nonprofit organization cannot have profits, i.e., net earnings.

It needs to be emphasized, too, that the prohibition against net earnings inuring to the benefit of any individual does not prevent the organization paying compensation for services rendered in the administration of the organization's activities. Obviously the greater the size of an organization, the larger its receipts, the greater the amounts of compensation that are warranted. In fact, the very presence of net earnings from an organization's operation would contribute toward making relatively large amounts of compensation reasonable for services rendered to that particular organization.

While it might appear to be a good thing for the various nonprofit organizations to at least break even, or to have net earnings, such does not happen to be the case. This conclusion observes the practical side, which is that too many nonprofit organizations have become too well endowed with financial resources in relation to their needs for a limited-purpose activity. And this oversupply of resources has been used to inflict highly destructive competition upon that sector of the economy that has the responsibility of producing physical goods and consumer-wanted services.

To explain this destructive competition let us start by saying that well-paying jobs with nonprofit organizations are more attractive than those with organizations that are supposed to operate at a profit. Obviously, employees of a nonprofit organization need not be concerned about their employer being able to have low costs so as to be able to meet the prices of a competitor. That this relaxes time schedules and work performance should be obvious. Now, of course, if the employer that produces goods and services wants to survive, he must meet the competition of the nonprofit sector in striving to get, and to keep, capable employees. This can only mean that the employer producing goods and services has had to incur higher costs and, of course, this has increased the prices for goods and services that the consumer has had to pay.

Further, the spending by nonprofit organizations is completely identical to that of the Federal Government. In each case, the spending increases the supply of money and credit (the demand), but contributes very little to the available goods and services (the supply). Identical, too, is the increase in inflation (i.e., price increases) that this brings.

There is one other factor of identity between nonprofit organizations and the Federal Government that customarily escapes notice: they are both monopolistic and are immune to competitive factors applying to business ventures. This means that nonprofit organizations are not subject to disciplines applying to business operations, and for the most part they need not bother about laws and regulations that apply to those who produce goods and services. That the unfair contest between monopoly and competitive enterprise would cause the production of goods and services to be reduced, and to increase the inflationary price spiral, should be apparent.

As uncontrolled monopolies, supported by tax-deductible dollars, nonprofit organizations have reflected the general American prosperity philosophy in that they have become quite materialistic. They have acquired costly real estate, they have built rather elaborate structures for office facilities, and they have considerably expanded their staffs of employees and administrators. There are even instances where a particular organization has actually accomplished the purpose for which it had been organized, and the organization promptly undertook new ventures rather than dismiss its staff and discontinue accepting contributions. The facts clearly show that there are in this nation many thousands of persons who have become professionals in the art of nonproductivity.

That this flow of contributions would ultimately also affect the operation of charities, as distinguished from other nonprofit tax-qualified organizations, was merely a matter of time. The manner in which this has become apparent can best be expressed by my repeating some comments I have overheard.

For example, I overheard the following dialogue recently between two businessmen, starting with Mr. X inquiring of Mr. Y, "Joe, you seem to have adopted a hard attitude toward charities lately. Do you want to deny charities the money they need?" Mr. Y thought a

111

moment and then replied, "Fred, it isn't that I don't want to help charities, but I have noticed that the offices of some charities are fancier than mine." And Mr. Y went on to say, "Not too many years ago, charities were willing to conduct their operations out of usable but outmoded buildings located close to the poorer sections of town where their help was needed, and then they were most willing to accept our used office furniture and equipment. But today charities are competing with business for choice locations, and they are competing for first-grade employees, including college graduates. Today one would not dare contribute used furniture to help equip their fancy offices, staffed by college graduates." Mr. Y concluded with the remark, "Somehow, I feel that charity has lost sight of its objective, which should be to help others."

As another example, a physician with years of experience in the practice of medicine was asked, "Dr. A, would you recommend our corporation making a contribution to the Society for the Prevention of (name of disease)?" Dr. A replied, "Most of these organizations accomplish some good, but they seem to spend a lot more money than should be needed for the limited amount of good that they do accomplish. Too much of the money contributed to charity is being spent for salaries for their expanding adminstrative staffs and for land and office buildings. And bear in mind they get quite a bit of free services from volunteer workers." Dr. A paused a moment and went on to say, "As a matter of fact, I could offer the same comment about hospitals these days, because hospitals are getting so expansion-minded you begin to wonder whether they have lost sight of their real purpose, which is to administer to the needs of the sick."

And another businessman, upon being asked why a hospital-planning committee was necessary, replied, "If you don't place any control on the building of new hospitals, you will soon have one hospital per city block, and the excessive cost of duplicate facilities would be positively staggering. Somehow these hospital fellows seem so interested in constructing new buildings and in buying very costly sophisticated equipment that they seem to have forgotten about the objective of 'treating the sick.' "

However, perhaps an attorney described the problem in better

112

fashion by stating, "We are spending more for charity, and we are having more crime; we are spending fortunes on education, and we have fewer skilled persons and more poor; we are showering millions upon hospitals, and it is getting to the point where a worker with good earnings must work one full week to cover the cost of one day in a hospital bed. Something has gone wrong."

The attorney's remark about the skyrocketing cost of hospital service should remind one that this nation's hospitals have been among the beneficiaries of the increase in charitable contributions. And at about the same time that this increase in contributions to hospitals occurred, the hospitals were also receiving a financial benefit from another source. This latter source provided for the payment of hospital charges for services through the hospitalization-insurance route. Although hospital-care insurance had been initiated in the early 1940s, it was not until employers began to pay a part or all of the hospitalization-insurance cost of their employees that this factor had any perceptible effect, from the standpoint that hospitals could consider the payment of their bills practically a certainty. (And it should be borne in mind that where most of the nation's employers contribute toward the hospitalization-insurance cost of their employees, this can only result in increasing the cost of business generally.) This means, of course, that the cost of hospitalization insurance has become a part of the prices that the consumer pays.

The American public has been told through advertisements of the organizations supplying hospitalization-insurance coverage that the upward spiraling of charges for hospital care has been caused by the hospitals being required to purchase expensive new equipment. This is, of course, a valid explanation. Nevertheless, one might question whether there has not occurred a change in attitude as to the equipment that is truly needed, once the hospitals had larger amounts of money to spend for new equipment. At the very least, one could suspect that in recent years a shortage of funds has not restricted the purchases of hospital equipment to that which was most essential.

The explanations concerning the increases in hospital-care charges also customarily omit any comment concerning the tremendous increases in salaries and wages paid by hospitals. Again, one has a right

113

to assume that the increases in compensation paid by hospitals have not been restricted by any lack of funds for this purpose.

However, there are several other facts that have been omitted from the explanations of hospitalization-insurance carriers as to the causes for the increases in hospital-care charges. For one thing, the insurance organizations do not explain that their own cost of operation has expanded with practically no restrictions, since these insurance carriers could expect the employer insuring his employees to pay whatever cost has been incurred, and, of course, the employers have in turn had this cost reimbursed by their customers, the consuming public, in the form of higher prices. Equally important, the hospitalization-insurance companies do not acknowledge that at least a part of the increases in the charges for hospitalization is caused by the fact that some hospitals now charge enough for their services to produce a profit from their operations, whereas at one time practically all hospitals operated on a break-even, or even on a loss basis.

This conversion of some hospitals from a nonprofit to a profit basis of operation has also not been made clear to the public. As a matter of fact, those hospitals having a profit have not advertised the fact in the reports they have issued. For example, the recent annual report of one particular hospital revealed that the total receipts and total expenditures balanced to the dollar. This should lead to the logical assumption that this hospital had operated on a nonprofit status. However, it could have been noted that not all of the expenditures were also expenses as this term is ordinarily understood. The expenditures listed in the report included the following:

Payment on long-term indebtedness	$ 548,016
New equipment and building remodeling	914,595
Increase in working capital	880,903
Total	$2,343,514

Anyone experienced in computing net income from a business operation would know that not one of the three items listed above could qualify as an expense, and none could be deducted in computing the net income of a taxable organization. Presumably, one might argue that the cost of new equipment and building remodeling was a valid expense for an organization that could not depreciate (deduct as expense) the annual estimated erosion of the cost of buildings and equipment. However, in this particular instance the annual report of the hospital had already included among expenditures a deduction for depreciation in the amount of $1,024,606. Hence, according to this hospital's report the erosion of the cost of past fixed-asset purchases was being charged against current income. As a matter of fact, one might even insist that where a nonprofit organization had acquired its facilities through donations (i.e., at no cost to the organization) there is some question whether depreciation could constitute a valid expense.

The total of the three expenditures as listed represented an increase in net worth of the hospital, which is the same as saying that they were items of profit rather than expense. An approximation of the annual profit (or net income) of this hospital can be computed, if we reduce the total $2,343,514 addition to net worth by the donations included in the receipts, the amount of donations being $203,-475. Applying simple arithmetic, one could conclude that the receipts of this hospital had exceeded expenditures by some $2,140,039, and in the business world this amount would be considered as net income or net profit.

Another hospital, located in the same community as the first, also issued an annual report in which revenues and expenses apparently balanced (as in the case of the other hospital) so as to support the assumption of a nonprofit operating status. But among the expenditures listed by the second hospital there was included the following item:

We charged operations for a pro-rated portion of the cost of our buildings and equipment . . . $1,347,000

This apparently served as the equivalent of some sort of depreciation.

However, this second hospital at least acknowledged that the total expenditures listed did not offset completely the total revenues, because under total expenditures was included the entry:

The balance was used for debt retirement and for new equipment and
services to obtain the best patient care . . . $841,000

Hence, it is logical to conclude that the second hospital, too, had
experienced a profit—at least this would be the result obtained by
applying the same rules for determining profit as apply to taxable
business firms.

The review of the two hospital annual reports does not in any way
imply that these hospitals had operated illegally in making a profit.
Let us remember that the Internal Revenue Code itself acknowledges that a nonprofit organization may profit, the only prohibition
in the Code being:

No part of the net earnings of which inures to the benefit of any private
shareholder or individual.

The two hospitals whose figures have been the subject of comment
and interpretation had no problem in meeting this version of a nonprofit operation, since they have no private shareholders. And the
possibility of their net earnings inuring to the benefit of any "individual" could be dismissed, too, because their "net earnings" do not
benefit any individual, at least not directly as profit would benefit a
shareholder. Accordingly, the profit in each case was available to
expand the hospitals additionally, and experience should tell us that
this use could, most likely, also expand hospital costs and the charges
made for hospital care.

The fact that hospitals have been getting quite a bit of publicity
from the surgical miracles taking place in their facilities reminds us
that hospitals serve the primary purpose of providing a place where
surgery can be performed and where the patient can recover after
surgery. Another reason why we need hospitals is to provide a place
where babies can be born. Lastly, there is the matter of needing a
hospital for emergencies, and for those with a serious illness that does
not involve surgery. Since quite a number of hospitals refuse to
supply emergency care on the ground that this can be better provided at some publicly operated facility especially established to
handle emergencies, we shall conclude that these emergency situa-

116

tions no longer are a primary purpose for providing hospital care. This leads to the conclusion that hospitals are primarily necessary for the purposes of surgical care, maternity care, and for the care of those with serious illness.

Obviously, as the number of cases requiring surgery or involving maternity or serious illness have expanded, there was a need to expand the number and size of hospitals. The annual report of one of the hospitals whose income has been the subject of comment in the preceding pages revealed the avenues by which that particular hospital had expanded its services. This was in the form of statistics covering ten-year intervals, viz:

TABLE 35

	Patients Admitted		Surgical	X-ray	Laboratory
	Adults	Newborn	Procedures	Procedures	Procedures
1928	1,529	251	1,105	607	3,012
1938	3,898	751	2,105	1,200	10,206
1948	6,682	1,648	4,419	8,012	47,225
1958	9,843	1,842	5,051	27,871	123,555
1968	14,457	1,942	5,750	53,706	389,483

By the simple process of adding the number of newborn patients admitted for each of the years to the number of surgical procedures for that year, we can obtain the total of the patients admitted for either maternity or surgery for that year. And if we then divide the number of surgical procedures plus the newborn patients by the total adult patients admitted for each particular year, we can ascertain the proportion of patients admitted for these two essential purposes. Table 36 is the result of the computation at the ten-year intervals.

Viewing these figures in another way, it is seen that over the past twenty years the adult patients that were admitted to this particular hospital, who required neither surgery nor maternity care, represented the following proportions of the total adult patients admitted:

1948	9%
1958	30%
1968	47%

117

TABLE 36

Year	Ratio of Surgical Procedures Plus Newborn to Total Adult Patients Admitted	Year	Ratio of Surgical Procedures Plus Newborn to Total Adult Patients Admitted
1928	89%	1958	70%
1938	73%	1968	53%
1948	91%		

Now, of course, the X-ray procedures and laboratory procedures as listed in the statistical tabulations attest to the fact that this hospital had patients other than bed patients, the term "outpatients" being generally applied. It is also to be recognized that hospital facilities are now being employed to a much greater extent for the various forms of mental illness and for diseases related to age and, of course, these would not be included in the statistics for surgical procedures or those for newborn babies. However, are multi-million-dollar hospital facilities needed for all of these other purposes? It surely would appear that a large portion of these other patients could be served under more economical conditions.

Unfortunately, however, the public cannot be concerned about these developments concerning hospitals because most of the patients in today's hospitals are not paying for their hospital stay. The cost is borne by hospitalization insurance. But, actually, this should cause more public concern over what hospitals are doing. This is so because the greater part of hospital-care insurance cost is paid for by employers, and this cost ends up in the prices the consumers pay. Accordingly, the public has every reason to be concerned.

This concludes the summary explanation of how nonprofit activity has contributed to inflating the economy. When this is coupled with government spending, we have ample reason to understand why prices have skyrocketed and why the purchasing power of the American dollar has slumped badly. However, the private and productive sector of the economy has also contributed enormously toward wrecking the value of the dollar. The explanation of how this has taken place will be given in succeeding chapters.

CHAPTER 8

The Deceptive Image of Continuously Increasing Productivity

The American public undoubtedly has noted that a tremendous amount of money is being expended on nonproductive government enterprise and on nonprofit-organization activity. That Federal Government spending of and by itself has been feeding inflation has not only been known by a number of persons but has also been the subject of critical comment by the more conservative segment of the public. Nevertheless, there is little evidence of a public demand that this overemphasis upon nonproductive spending be stopped.

To expect the public to object to the spending is to hope for a miracle. For one thing, the public does not know that spending on nonproductive pursuits is retarding the necessary increase in the production of goods and services needed by the consumer. And the public could not know this, because Americans have been told that they, as a people, are attaining ever higher levels of national productivity.

Hence, there exists in America an economic phenomenon in that a people with a mounting rate of productivity are nevertheless experiencing continuously increasing price levels for the goods and services they want to purchase. Obviously, the measurement of productivity has to be at fault, because there can be no question about the continuously increasing prices portion of this economic riddle.

It is unfortunate that the public has been given little, if any, information concerning the measuring stick that is used to support the conclusion that national productivity has been continuously expanding. The only information furnished consists of the regular publication of the estimates of an ever-increasing Gross National Product, more often simply referred to as "GNP."

Before getting into the matter of what GNP really means, it is appropriate to explain first that the Federal bureaucracy has developed a procedure of officially defining words and terms for particular governmental purposes that often invites a public misunderstanding. This consists of the bureaucracy taking a commonly used term and then, by official definition, providing a meaning for bureaucratic use that is different from the common meaning. That this process can actively misinform the public should be taken for granted.*

The definition for GNP, "Gross National Product," is contained in the *U.S. Bureau of the Census, Statistical Abstract of the United States: 1965* (page 322), which states:

> Gross national product—Gross national product (called GNP) represents the total national output of goods and services at market prices. It measures this output in terms of the expenditures by which the goods and services are acquired. The expenditures comprise purchases of goods and services by consumers and government, gross private domestic investment, and net exports of goods and services. The goods and services included in GNP are, for the most part, those actually bought for final use (excluding illegal transactions) in the markets. There are a number of inclusions, however, which represent imputed values, the most important of which is the rental value of owner-occupied dwellings. GNP, the total national output, also measures the product attributable to the factors of production—labor and property —supplied by residents of the United States or paid in indirect taxes.

*For example, in 1934 Congress enacted a statute providing for Federal Savings and Loan Associations, and the law required that these associations obtain their capital funds only through a sale of their shares of stock. However, in 1949 the Federal Home Loan Bank Board thought it wise to encourage investment in these associations by defining "savings accounts" as the share capital of these associations, thus permitting the public to believe they were depositing funds in a savings account, when in fact the investment was in shares of stock.

GNP differs from "national income," described below, mainly in that GNP includes allowances for depreciation and similar capital consumption and for indirect taxes (such as sales and excise taxes).

The definition starts out logically, and with an image of respectability, with the statement that GNP represents total national output of goods and services at market prices. However, then the definition proceeds to take for granted that an estimate of all expenditures made for goods and services accomplishes the same result as computing the total national output of these at market prices. Since GNP is an estimate of the total expenditures made for goods and services by both consumers and the government, plus a few other items, one must conclude that GNP is really nothing more than an estimate of total national spending rather than any reliable measurement of national productivity.

Perhaps the supporters of the GNP approach to measuring productivity may want to insist that where expenditures have been made for the purchases of goods and services, these goods and services must have been produced prior to their purchase. Admittedly, any goods and services that have been purchased had to be produced first. But it does not ordinarily follow that the production of goods and services occurs simultaneously with their purchase. In many instances goods are purchased long after they were produced. Nor does it follow that all services should be given equal significance in measuring the type of productivity that is necessary for human survival. One has the right to suspect that when the public receives glowing reports of increasing productivity, it has in mind the productivity that is necessary to support and maintain human beings.

Perhaps I can offer my criticism of the GNP measurement in understandable fashion by referring to some hypothetical examples. As the first example, I mention the fact that for quite a number of years the national television networks have spent millions of dollars for the right to rerun movies originally filmed as early as the 1930s. Obviously the actual productivity related to producing these films occurred in the 1930s, and the expenditures related to the filming must have been included in GNP at that time. Nevertheless, were the

121

millions spent for the right to show these films again, years later, included in productivity (GNP)? As another illustration, the fantastic sums that have been expended on the purchase of antiques and art objects can be mentioned. Were these expenditures considered a part of national productivity over and over again each time that these antiques and art objects were resold at higher prices, regardless of the fact that the items traded were actually produced decades, if not centuries, earlier? Then, on the matter of imputed values included in GNP, we can mention the case of an owner-occupied dwelling originally constructed in 1935 at a cost of $8,000, and which had a market value of about $20,000 in 1965. In what way could the greatly increased (inflated) rental value of this dwelling contribute toward the national productivity as measured for 1965?

It stands to reason that under this measurement of productivity the Federal Government, the satellite state and local governments, and the many thousands of nonprofit organizations are treated quite kindly. Under the GNP definition, all of the billions of dollars spent by these organizations are treated as the equivalent of the production of consumer goods and services. Yes, the billions of expenditures by these nonproducers serve to increase productivity (GNP) even though the expenditures merely kite demand (purchasing power) for consumer goods and services without, at the same time, contributing an iota to the supply of these. Hence, the GNP measurement of productivity serves to hide the effects of inflation by the simple process of computing a synthetic productivity that at all times precisely equals the inflated purchasing power. This prompts the sarcastic observation that had this GNP measurement been in use at the time of the post-World War I inflation in Germany, then Germany would have been experiencing the highest productivity imaginable, in spite of the fact that it required the proverbial billion German marks to buy a single loaf of bread!

Perhaps this synthetic version of productivity would have caused a minimum of actual damage had its application been restricted to keeping Americans satisfied from a psychological standpoint. Unfortunately, however, this highly questionable approach in measuring national productivity has been used as the basis for determining that wage increases are necessary. In other words, as the workers' productivity is presumed to increase each year, the workers' compensation has to be adjusted upward to compensate for the increased productivity. Hence, as national spending increases, the GNP moves upward to signify an increased worker productivity, and this requires wages to be increased to shove GNP even higher. Accordingly, there is set in motion a vicious cycle of wage rates chasing after spending.

Since the government sees to it that liberal quantities of spending money are always available, the public has never fully comprehended that such prosperity is artificial and that its continuation depends entirely upon the government using a large part of the workers' earnings (the income tax part) to keep money and credit (the demand) consistently in excess of the available goods and services (the supply).

No matter how the public is deluded by this image of great productivity and prosperity, the published GNP figures, if carefully analyzed, provide at least a hint of the way in which the delusion has been accomplished. But in order to demonstrate that fact we must first establish a few ground rules as to the type of productivity that is most needed to furnish humans with the basic needs for survival. We shall employ somewhat the same approach that had been employed during World War II and used to determine which men could be drafted for the armed forces and which men were needed in jobs "at home" for the essential purpose of either aiding war production or supplying the most essential of basic human necessities.

However, in measuring peacetime productivity we shall not restrict the needed productivity to cover only the bare "necessities" of life. In other words, instead of looking into economic activity to determine what is needed to support people at minimum levels, and yet produce the utmost in war goods (as we did during World War II), this time we shall focus attention on the type of economic activity that best supports people during time of peace. Referring to the several production categories used by the United States Department of Commerce in estimating GNP, we proceed to apply a logical approach in determining the type of productivity that is most

123

needed, and to segregate the GNP categories into "productive" and "nonproductive" groups, viz:

Productive	Nonproductive
Manufacturing	Wholesale and retail trade
Contract construction	Finance, insurance and
Public utilities	real estate
Transportation	Government and governmental
Communications	enterprises
Mining	Services
Agriculture	

In making this distinction, we are not concluding that those activities listed under "nonproductive" are not needed, because they are needed. However, they are not really needed to the same extent as those listed under "productive." As a matter of fact, the activities listed as nonproductive are parasitical in that their very existence depends for survival upon the activities in the productive categories.

It should be noted that services have been included in the nonproductive group, even though many services are needed by consumers and purchased by consumers directly no differently than consumer products. Nevertheless, the service industry has become involved to a major extent in serving other industrial classifications, rather than restricted to serving the consumer. This is particularly the case in the fields of law, accounting and the various forms of consulting work. Hence, services should logically be included with the parasitical, the nonproductive, group. To explain that logic, a large part of the activities of the services industry is not supplied at the request of consumers, but at the request of industry, commerce and the government. Yet the cost of these activities are included in the prices the consumer pays for whatever he does purchase. Incidentally, this same conclusion would apply to most of the "industries" listed under the "nonproductive" column, i.e., the consumer pays for these without much selection or choice on his part.

As a matter of fact, except for those activities in the nonproductive sector that are, in limited quantities, separately ordered and paid for directly by consumers, the cost of all of the nonproductive activities

124

could best be described as representing the "overhead costs" of the national economy. Like the overhead costs of an individual business, these nonproductive costs of the entire economy must be included in the national price structure. Though necessary in many respects, this overhead activity cannot increase to disproportionate levels (in relation to productive activity) without immediately being reflected in increased prices for those goods and services that are wanted by the consumer.

Having decided which economic activities are productive and which nonproductive, we next proceed to analyze the increases in these activities in terms of GNP. The period used to measure the increase shall be from 1947, by which year the United States had completed the conversion to a peacetime economy, to the more recent year of 1970. Using the U.S. Department of Commerce GNP estimates, the comparison follows:

TABLE 37

INCREASE IN GROSS NATIONAL PRODUCT
IN CURRENT DOLLARS BY INDUSTRY,
COMPARING 1970 WITH 1947

| Industry | Gross National Product | | Increase in GNP 1970 vs. |
	1947	1970	1947
	(in billions of dollars)		
Agriculture, forestry and fisheries	20.8	30.8	10.0
Mining	6.8	16.8	10.0
Contract construction	8.8	45.8	37.0
Manufacturing	66.9	253.2	186.3
Wholesale and retail trade	43.4	167.3	123.9
Finance, insurance and real estate	22.7	133.7	111.0
Transportation	13.6	38.2	24.6
Communications	3.1	22.5	19.4
Public utilities	3.8	22.3	18.5
Services	20.4	114.3	93.9
Government and government enterprises	19.2	128.8	109.6
Rest of the world	0.8	4.6	3.8
Total Gross National Product	231.3	974.1	742.8

Source: U. S. Department of Commerce.

125

The foregoing data reveal how much "productivity" of value to the consumer is contained in the GNP figures that support the image of an increasing national productivity. Using our categories of productive and nonproductive activity, between 1947 and 1970 the changes in the GNP of these groups have been as follows:

| | The Increase in Productive and Nonproductive GNP | |
	Productive GNP	Nonproductive GNP
1947 Total	125.6 billions (or 54.5% of total GNP)	105.7 billions (or 45.5% of total GNP)
Increase between 1947 and 1970	302.0 billions (or 40.7% of increase)	440.8 billions (or 59.3% of increase)
1970 Total	427.6 billions (or 43.9% of total GNP)	546.5 billions (or 56.1% of total GNP)

These figures furnish at least the suggestion that, in terms of the GNP figures, the nonproductive expenditures have outstripped productive expenditures despite the much-advertised image of increased productivity. Nevertheless, these GNP statistics merely scratch the surface in revealing how badly the actual productivity of goods and services wanted by the consumer have been curtailed. The reason for this is that the GNP statistics estimate the supposed end result of spending, but the statistics do not reveal the source of the spending. Neither do the GNP figures touch upon the important factor of the changes in numbers of workers, upon comparing productive with nonproductive activity.

For example, the GNP figures of the Department of Commerce estimate the "productivity" of all "Government and government enterprises" as being only $128.8 billion for 1970, which is really a small amount for all state, local and Federal Government activity. However, the total expenditures of the Federal Government *alone* for 1970 could be estimated at about $210.6 billion, or substantially more than the GNP attributed to all government enterprise. Please note, incidentally, that the figure of $210.6 billion, estimated as the total spending by the Federal Government for 1970, amounted to over 83 percent of the total GNP of the entire manufacturing industry for 1970, as the latter amount was estimated by the Department of Commerce. Hence, by the process of fragmenting Federal Government spending into industry purchases for the purpose of estimating GNP by industries, there is effectively hidden once again any reliable estimate of the productivity that was purchased by American consumers.

Meanwhile, the American consumer has been told that a cessation of American war activities, coupled with a curb of Federal Government defense expenditures, will quickly mend the current economic difficulties and cause the price increases to be reversed. It is relatively simple to expose the emptiness of that wishful thought. I shall start by computing an estimate of Federal Government nondefense spending for recent years. Here is that tabulation:

TABLE 38

COMPUTATION OF
FEDERAL GOVERNMENT NONDEFENSE SPENDING

Fiscal Years Ended June 30th	Federal Government Expenditures Including Aid to State and Local Governments*	Less National Defense Expenditures**	Federal Government Expenditures Excluding National Defense Expenditures***
	(billions of dollars)		
1960	97.3	45.7	51.6
1961	104.9	47.5	57.4
1962	113.4	51.1	62.3
1963	118.8	52.8	66.0
1964	125.9	54.2	71.7
1965	130.1	50.2	79.9
1966	143.0	57.7	85.3
1967	166.8	70.2	96.6

Sources: *U.S. Bureau of the Census.
**Bureau of the Budget.
***The result of subtraction.

The foregoing amply demonstrates how Federal Government spending had almost doubled over a seven-year period *even after all defense expenditures have been eliminated* from the Government spending total. Of course, the American consumer might expect some relief from spiraling prices if some fraction of the $50 billion-plus of total annual defense expenditures could be eliminated and turned into the production of consumer goods and services. However, why should the American consumer be expected to wait for a curbing of defense expenditures in order to get price relief when the facts show that in each of recent years the Federal Government's total annual *nondefense* expenditures have exceeded the total annual wages paid to all production workers in all manufacturing industries in the United States. Here is that compilation:

TABLE 39

FEDERAL GOVERNMENT NONDEFENSE SPENDING
vs.
TOTAL WAGES PAID ALL PRODUCTION WORKERS

Fiscal Years Ended June 30th*	Federal Government Expenditures (Excluding National Defense Expenditures)**	Total Wages Paid All Production Workers in all Manufacturing Industries (Excluding Hand and Neighborhood Industries)***
	(billions of dollars)	
1960	51.6	55.5
1961	57.4	54.7
1962	62.3	59.1
1963	66.0	62.1
1964	71.7	65.8
1965	79.9	71.1
1966	85.3	78.3
1967	96.6	81.0

*Calendar Years for Wages Paid to Production Workers
Sources: **Computation heretofore explained.
***U.S. Bureau of the Census.

These facts concerning government nondefense spending vs. the wages paid all production workers in all manufacturing plants can be illustrated even more clearly by noting that, except for these nondefense Federal expenditures, the American economy could readily have paid the wages for twice the number of production workers actually employed in all manufacturing plants.*And there would be

*As here used, the term "production workers" means just that. This does not include office, administrative, or supervisory personnel.

nothing invalid about that suggestion, because the costs of these nondefense expenditures of the government, no differently than the costs of wages paid to the production workers, had to be included in the prices the consumer has had to pay. Meanwhile, those in the Federal Government, including the representatives of the American people in the Congress and in the Senate, have claimed that they were giving the problem of increasing prices a first priority!

The statistics presented in this chapter may be somewhat boring to you. Nevertheless, some additional statistics are necessary to provide rather overwhelming evidence that the GNP image of a greatly increased productivity is completely misleading, if not wholly inaccurate.

At this point we shall examine the employment statistics. After all, if America has become increasingly more productive, some evidence of this should be reflected in the number of persons employed in productive activity. Hence, we turn to the Bureau of Labor Statistics reports as to the number of persons employed in nonagricultural employment, excluding proprietors, self-employed, domestic servants, unpaid family workers, and members of the armed forces. As so restricted, the persons employed in 1950, 1960, and July 1968 were reported as follows:

TABLE 40

PERSONS EMPLOYED IN
VARIOUS WORK CATEGORIES

	July 1968	1960	1950
Employment:		(000)	
Manufacturing	19,822	16,796	15,241
Mining	633	712	901
Contract construction	3,181	2,885	2,333
Transportation and public utilities	4,337	4,004	4,034
Trade	14,094	11,391	9,386
Finance, insurance and real estate	3,346	2,669	1,919
Services	10,495	7,423	5,382
Government	12,248	8,353	6,026
	68,156	54,234	45,222

Source: Bureau of Labor Statistics.

129

In analyzing these figures, we shall use the same "productive" and "nonproductive" categories as were used in analyzing GNP data. As so grouped, the number of persons employed can be restated as follows:

TABLE 41

	July 1968	1960	1950
		(000)	
Total employees in "productive employment" (manufacturing, mining, contract construction, transportation and public utilities)	27,973	24,397	22,509
Total employees in "nonproductive employment" (trade, finance, insurance, real estate, services, government)	40,183	29,836	22,713
Percentage of nonproductive employment to productive employment	144%	122%	101.0%

These Bureau of Labor Statistics figures reveal that, between 1950 and July 1968, productive employees increased only 24.4 percent, whereas nonproductive employees increased by a whopping 77 percent. This disproportion hardly supports the belief that America as a nation could be attaining an ever-higher productivity *in consumer products*. As a matter of fact, the gargantuan increase in nonproductive employment provides only a pilot-run sample of the actual *total decline* in productive work activity.

The last conclusion refers to the fact that the well-advertised image of a certain prosperity has caused all American workers, including those characterized as being in productive work, to be something less than good producers. Jobs have been plentiful and employers have been in no position to insist upon good worker performance. Meanwhile, American business enterprise paid no attention to the scarcity in the numbers of trained, experienced and competent employees, but expanded to make the scarcity even more serious. That this could only lead to an upgrading of employees so that job titles

130

denoting expertise became meaningless should have been taken for granted.* The foregoing conclusions, however, cannot be substantiated by statistics and this is another factor that has prevented any challenge to the publicized image of an ever-increasing national productivity. Nevertheless, there is available one slight datum that demonstrates quite clearly how job titles became meaningless. I refer to a literal population explosion in secretaries, and a famine in the number of typists and stenographers, viz:

TABLE 42

NUMBER OF STENOGRAPHERS, TYPISTS AND SECRETARIES

	1950	1960
Stenographers	416,844	264,157
Typists	339,875	516,844
Secretaries	781,324	1,451,639

Source: U.S. Department of Commerce, Bureau of the Census.

Anyone highly dependent upon a female skilled in the art of taking dictation and typing (such as those in the field of court reporting) can attest to the fact that persons so skilled are scarce despite the increase in the number of would-be secretaries. As a matter of fact, although skill in dictation and typing could command high levels of compensation, the alleged secretaries consider employment at this skill as demeaning and lacking "challenge."

But let us not restrict the inclination of workers to be "chiefs" rather than "Indians" only to female employees. This idiosyncrasy is prevalent in all forms of work, and at all levels of performance. For example, law school graduates have to be promised a future law-firm-partnership status before they even work long enough to demonstrate that they are qualified to be lawyers. And many accountants accept employment only if they are assured that they will soon be vice-presidents of finance, even though in many cases they have had

*There was one exception to the process of attempting to improve worker performance with a fancier title, and this took place in the professional sports area. There, the expansion in number of teams was accompanied by a "drafting" of players from other teams. Apparently, competent sports performers were more scarce than competent persons that could direct American business and financial affairs.

131

little or no experience in the basic principles of accounting, and know practically nothing about finance.*

Meanwhile, the passionate desire for everyone to become a "chief" is reflected in the expansion of this nation's institutions of higher learning. According to *The Morgan Guaranty Survey* for June 1971, the annual budgets for these institutions soared from $4 billion in 1955 to an estimated $27 billion for 1971. This *Survey* also tells us that Federal funds to higher schools swelled from $500 million in 1955 to $4.4 billion in 1968. Obviously, this expansion and spending created a competition for professors, and many college graduates decided to follow this nonproductive pursuit for earning a living rather than enter the "rat race" of other employment.

The foregoing statistics and comment provide only a short synopsis of why full employment is not necessarily productive, and as to why the huge increase in number of employees has merely increased costs and kited prices.

Meanwhile, those in state, local and Federal governments professed a great concern over "inflation" and spiraling prices. Perhaps their concern about inflation could have been mitigated had they kept the number of government employees under control. But, instead of doing that, they permitted an increase in government employment between 1950 and July 1968 that exceeded the increase in all productive employment categories combined. Here are those figures:

TABLE 43

	Increase in Number of Persons 1950 to July 1968
Employment in manufacturing, mining, contract construction, transportation and public utilities	5,464,000
Employment in government	6,222,000

Nevertheless, the economic experts would have you believe that the expansion of the number of employees in nonmanufacturing

*The shortcomings of those bearing fancy job titles lie hidden during rampant inflation-fed prosperity. While profits flow, the performance of everyone looks good. Nevertheless, beginning with the close of the 1960s, many corporations began to experience difficulties and the "heads began to roll."

activity is a wonderful development. They reason that this is what has kept a large number of persons employed in the face of a contraction in manufacturing employment caused by mass production and automation. Of course it is a desirable objective to keep as many persons employed as possible. But what makes the economic experts so certain that manufacturing activity (and the employees in that activity) has been expanded to its utmost expansion potential, so as to make this obvious overexpansion of nonmanufacturing activity necessary? And this question should be followed with the suggestion that one should doubt that American manufacturing has been expanded to its full potential when huge volumes of foreign-made goods—often having better quality, providing greater selectivity, and available at a lower price—have been imported into this nation. Have the economic experts reckoned with the possibility that easy money (and with jobs easy to get) has unduly expanded nonmanufacturing activity so as to stultify American manufacturing growth and development?

The foregoing reference to the importation of foreign-made goods prompts the suggestion that the excessive American expansion in nonproductive activity is directly related to the United States balance-of-payments-deficit problem. Perhaps this can be clarified by raising the following question:

> How do Americans intend to export American productivity represented by wholesale and retail trade, by finance, insurance and real estate, by Government and Government enterprises, and by the services, so as to counterbalance (pay for by offset) the increasing imports by Americans of foreign-made goods?

If that question should be difficult to answer, there is an alternative question that may prove even more troublesome, and that is:

> How do Americans intend ultimately to pay for the excess of American imports of foreign goods over American exports to foreign nations, when foreigners already hold American dollars in an amount well in excess of the American gold supply, which is only about $11 billion.

A classical example of the tremendous growth in service employment that has little or no connection with the production of goods or services that the consumer wants can be noted upon visiting

133

Washington, D.C. Of course, as soon as there is mention made of Washington, one can anticipate that a harangue will follow about the thousands of Federal bureaucrats based there who are supported by the taxpayers. But, in this particular instance, the reference to Washington does not concern government employees. Instead, I am directing attention to the large number of costly office structures built in Washington since the close of World War II, and that are tenanted by *nongovernment* enterprises.

Who are the tenants of these nongovernment office buildings located in Washington? All kinds of associations purporting to represent industry and business, trades, the sciences, medicine, education, the professions, and including, too, all kinds of consultants who furnish advice to those having to deal with the Federal Government. Of this vast quantity of nonproducers, looking only at those organizations that use the word "association" in their names, it requires some six pages of the Washington, D.C., telephone directory "yellow pages" to list them all.

Though it is repetition, it must be emphasized again that the consumer pays for the vast nongovernment group of employees based in Washington in a manner not too different from that by which he pays for the salaries of government employees. If the organization is a trade or business association, the cost is included in the prices charged the consumer by the business members of the association. In the case of scientific, educational and like associations, the consumer pays the cost, too, because these organizations are customarily supported by contributions of some business or profession that the consumer must patronize; hence once again the costs are a part of the prices that the consumer pays. Meanwhile, the American consumer is about to be rescued by several varieties of consumer organizations. Obviously, these will merely increase the nonproductive employment and the consumer will be loaded with the cost of them, too.

This chapter will close with a comment attributed to Henry Ford II, because the words credited to him express better than statistics the dilemma confronting America. Mr. Ford's observation was that, if present trends continue, the U.S. economy could become a "service economy" where, figuratively speaking, we would exist by "taking in one another's laundry."

CHAPTER 9

Why Tight Money Became Inevitable

As previously mentioned, the United States, at the close of World War II, was a nation whose people and business and financial institutions were reasonably well supplied with cash. For the most part, debts other than those of the Federal Government were relatively small in proportion to the liquid assets. Stated simply, this nation was financially liquid. Nevertheless, a little less than 25 years later—beginning with the year 1966—this same nation was in the throes of a tight-money dilemma, the exact opposite of financial liquidity.

Strangely enough, not too much has been publicly offered by way of explanation for this switch from a condition of high liquidity to tight money. Even more astounding, there was almost no admonition from this country's leadership that borrowing be curtailed, or any suggestion that debts be repaid. Instead of concern about the cause of tight money, this nation's leaders were arguing about who is responsible for the high interest costs of continued borrowing.*

The obvious reason for the tight-money predicament was that this nation had overspent and overborrowed to the point where the

---

*This can be compared to a hypothetical condition where a nation becomes addicted to alcoholism, but instead of seeking a cure for that, the nation's leadership complains about the rising costs of alcohol.

savings available for borrowing could no longer satisfy the borrowing demand. In fact, this condition was completely similar to that of the demand for goods and services exceeding the available supply. Whether we speak in terms of a shortage of goods, or a shortage of funds for borrowing, both must be reflected in higher costs for the items in short supply, i.e., higher prices and higher interest rates.

But at the time that the final effects of government overspending were being reflected in high prices and in high interest rates, some of the leaders of both political parties were disavowing any feeling of guilt. Although politicians once boasted that they had planned the economy, and once proudly proclaimed that "the Federal Government controlled interest rates," they began to stop mentioning these prior claims. Incidentally, they also neglected to mention the depression-bred laws that supposedly had provided the Federal Government with a firmer control over banking.

Perhaps these politicians were, in fact, admitting for the first time that when interest rates had been low, it had not been the Government that kept rates low. Instead, an abundance of funds available for borrowing had dictated the low interest rates.

Obviously, any claim that bankers were responsible for the soaring interest rates disregarded the important fact that the bankers were the "middlemen" between savers and borrowers. Equally obvious was the fact that the Federal Government, through its spending, had caused prices to inflate so as to require intensive borrowing to meet higher budgets of both the consumer and those in business.

Strange as it may seem, not only did the Federal Government, through its uncontrolled spending, promote a need for national borrowing, but the government also provided a direct encouragement for maximum private borrowing. I refer to the fact that the same Federal income tax that provided the funds for government spending, thus feeding inflationary price increases, also encouraged an indiscriminate borrowing.

The Federal income tax did this by allowing all interest expense to be deducted for income tax purposes, no matter for what purpose the borrowing was incurred. Obviously, Americans were encouraged to spend with borrowed funds under the condition that a part of the interest cost of the borrowing was "paid for" by the Government in the form of a reduction in the income tax. And the higher the borrower's income tax bracket, the greater the amount of taxes saved through borrowing. This tax incentive for borrowing was most attractive to those in business (and to speculators) who expected to increase their incomes with the use of borrowed funds, even before taking into account the tax saving related to the deduction of interest from taxable income.

As a matter of fact, stock speculators were actually provided with a double benefit under the income tax, if they used borrowed funds. Their gains from speculation received the low-taxed capital gain benefit.* Hence, by increasing the amount invested with borrowed funds so as to increase their expected gains, their interest expense was tax deductible *against fully taxed* (or so-called "ordinary") income, while their profits were subject to a low tax.

It is something of an anomaly to note that practically everyone knows that interest expense is tax deductible, yet this tax deduction is supported by no sound legal or economic reason. Interest incurred on nonbusiness loans is practically the only personal expense that is tax deductible. Somewhat similarly, interest incurred on business loans is the only cost of capital used in business that is tax deductible, i.e., dividends paid on capital invested in shares of stock are not tax deductible.

During the universal craze to borrow, there was one arm of the Federal Government—the Federal Reserve System—that did warn against overborrowing. However, one should not overlook the fact that this warning had developed a bit late—just before the condition of tight money had become completely obvious. The first noticeable warning was issued by the Federal Reserve when William McChesney Martin, Jr., Chairman of the Federal Reserve Board, publicly stated in the summer of 1965 that there were some "disquieting similarities" between the then-current economic conditions and those of the late 1920s.

Thereafter the Federal Reserve Bank of Chicago also complained

*Provided the amount speculated stayed in one place for more than six months.

about the borrowing by corporations—in July of 1966, just about the time that the tight-money development was already obvious. This was in the form of an article entitled "Corporate Cash—20-Year Decline" contained in the Chicago Reserve Bank's publication *Business Conditions,* from which the following paragraphs have been taken:

> Nonfinancial corporations held a record 66.5 billion dollars in liquid assets at the start of 1966, including currency, demand deposits, time deposits, Government securities and commercial paper of other corporations. Although at a new high in dollar amount, corporate liquid assets were at a postwar low relative to both liabilities and sales.
>
> During World War II many corporations reduced their debts and acquired an unprecedented volume of cash and Governments. Corporate liquid assets at the end of 1945 equaled 54 percent of total liabilities. In subsequent years liquid assets rose, but not nearly as fast as liabilities. This ratio had declined to 31 percent by the end of 1955. Then and since, some observers suggested that liquid asset holdings had reached a practical minimum for the efficient performance of the corporate sector. Nevertheless, the slide continued—to 23 percent in 1960 and less than 19 percent last year.
>
> During June of this year, corporations made accelerated payments of income and withholding taxes. They continue to finance record capital outlays and large increases in inventories and receivables. Increased borrowing from banks and in the capital markets reflect the need to supplement internally generated funds with outside financing. As in other times of money stringency, many corporations also have reduced bank balances and sold short-term liquid assets to meet bills that came due.*

There were, of course, other economic areas where debt had been increased. Consumer credit was an example. The author remembers well how the late Franklin Delano Roosevelt had expressed himself

---

*Those who find comfort in the fact that brokers' loans were at insignificant levels, so as to indicate that there was less borrowing against stock purchases than took place in 1929, might ask themselves this simple question: Does it really make investments in shares less hazardous when the corporations rather than the owners of the corporations—the shareholders—do the heavy borrowing?

quite forcibly on the point that installment purchasing by consumers was nothing more than a delusive process that had kept consumers poor, and had prompted the overspending in the palmy days of the 1920s. And since Roosevelt should be classed as the founder of the concept that the government should control the economy, one would assume that the Federal Government would have discouraged consumer credit. But this did not happen, since it might have adversely affected the prosperity about which the Federalists were boasting.

As a matter of fact, no lesser governmental authority than the Federal Reserve Board published monthly the facts concerning the unbelievable surge in consumer credit in its publication, *The Federal Reserve Bulletin*. Note what happened since the days of Franklin Delano Roosevelt:

TABLE 44

CONSUMER CREDIT
(in billions of dollars)

1939	7.22	1960	56.03
1941	9.17	1963	71.74
1945	5.66	1964	80.27
		1965	90.31
		1966	97.54
		1967	102.13
		1968	113.19

Source: *The Federal Reserve Bulletin.*

Through reading the pages of *The Federal Reserve Bulletin* one can note, too, how installment credit had attained an unbelievably high proportion of total consumer credit (Table 45).

One should not assume, however, that only the Federal Reserve Bank of Chicago or the national Federal Reserve Board had become concerned about the growth in debt; the Morgan Guaranty Trust Company was somewhat concerned, too. In any event, in that same month, July 1966, when the Federal Reserve Bank of Chicago had commented about the increase in corporate borrowings, the Morgan Guaranty Trust Company, in its publication, *The Morgan Guaranty Survey*, provided a historical record of the growth of government

TABLE 45

RATIO OF INSTALLMENT CREDIT TO
TOTAL CONSUMER CREDIT

1939	62.5%	1960	77.5%
1941	66.5%	1963	77.0%
1945	43.5%	1964	77.5%
		1965	78.5%
		1966	79.5%
		1967	79.5%
		1968	79.5%

Source: *The Federal Reserve Bulletin.*

and private debt since 1930. Here is that tabulation:

TABLE 46

GROSS DEBT IN THE UNITED STATES
(year end, billions of dollars)

	1930	1940	1945	1960	1965	% Increase 1960–65
Government	35.8	73.8	309.2	389.2	457.9	17.7
Federal	17.3	53.6	292.6	322.1	359.2	11.5
State and local	18.5	20.2	16.6	67.1	98.7	47.1
Private	178.5	142.0	154.1	648.0	992.8	53.2
Corporate	107.4	89.0	99.5	361.6	533.0	47.4
Noncorporate	71.1	53.0	54.6	286.4	459.8	60.5
Home mortgage and consumer credit	17.9*	24.8	23.4	190.2	290.1	52.5
Business property mortgages	14.1	9.6	9.3	40.2	82.5	105.2
Farm and other	39.1	18.6	21.9	56.0	87.2	55.7
Total government and private	214.3	215.8	463.3	1,037.2	1,450.7	39.9

*Mortgage debt only for 1930; consumer debt included with "other" debt for 1930.

Source: *Morgan Guaranty Survey* for July 1966.

Hence, at long last, and after something like twenty years of almost passionate spending and borrowing, there began to appear some telltale indications that national borrowing practices were at least being noticed. And during the long intervening period, the American public had been told that its borrowing practices were perfectly

140

satisfactory because America had unlimited resources and an expanding economy.

Recalling what has been said in prior pages of this text, to the effect that Americans had paid up their debts and were in a highly liquid (cash) position in 1945, at the close of World War II, let us note what these Americans did in the fifteen years after 1945 on the matter of borrowing:

TABLE 47

INCREASE IN DEBT FOR THE PERIOD 1945–1960

Federal Government	29.5 billion dollars
State and local governments	50.5 billion dollars
Private individuals and corporations	493.9 billion dollars
Total	573.9 billion dollars

Source: Computed from *Morgan Guaranty Survey* debt figures.

The foregoing figures indicate that in the relatively short space of fifteen years private individuals and corporations had gone into debt to the extent of almost one-half trillion dollars. Even more alarming was the fact that the growth in debt had substantially accelerated in the five years (1960–1965) succeeding this fifteen years of a borrowing mania. This can best be demonstrated by comparing the average annual increase in debt for groups other than the Federal Government for the period 1945–1960 with the annual increase in debt for these same groups for the later five-year period of 1960–1965 (Table 48).

But this explosive tempo of borrowing and the "tight money" condition of 1966 did not cause the economists in the public eye to become visibly shaken. They persisted in voicing the conclusion that this vast quantity of borrowing was normal when undertaken under the conditions of a growing or expanding national economy.

However, as with many trite expressions of recent vintage, the term "expanding national economy" is somewhat hollow and meaningless. Certainly increased spending of and by itself, which had been

141

TABLE 48

ACCELERATION IN ANNUAL DEBT INCREASES FOR GROUPS
OTHER THAN THE FEDERAL GOVERNMENT

	State & Local	Corporate	Home Mortgages & Consumers Credit	Business Mortgages	Farm & Other
Annual Average Increase 1945–1960 (stated in billions of dollars)	3.4	17.5	11.1	2.1	2.3
Average Annual Increase 1960–1965 (stated in billions of dollars)	6.3	34.3	20.0	8.5	6.2

Source: Computed from *Morgan Guaranty Survey* debt figures.

caused by following the price spiral upward, hardly justified an increase in borrowing. Nevertheless, if the increased borrowing was merely keeping pace with a real increase in wealth in terms of physical properties, then one had to acknowledge that there was some merit in the increased borrowing. I employ the term "real increase in wealth" to distinguish this from any synthetic increase in wealth resulting solely from the price increases.

The possibility that increased borrowing has been accompanied by an increase in wealth (physical goods) prompts an examination into the relationship between the growth in national debt with the increase in national wealth (physical properties). Of course, one should observe the precaution of considering only the real increase in wealth, i.e., not the increase caused by price inflation. The same *Morgan Guaranty Survey* published data on the growth in physical properties (wealth). This was supplied in the issue for August 1966, immediately after the issue of the *Survey* that contained the national debt statistics. From the August 1966 issue that provided an estimate of U.S. wealth, i.e., physical goods

and properties, we obtain the following information as to the growth
of that national wealth:

TABLE 49

WEALTH, PEOPLE AND PRODUCT

	1900	1929	1948	1958	1964
Total U.S. wealth:					
In current dollars (billions)	88	439	928	1,703	2,223
In constant 1947–49 dollars (billions)	315	778	883	1,244	1,481
Population (millions)	76.8	122.4	147.9	175.6	193.4
Per capita wealth:					
In current dollars	1,145	3,586	6,274	9,698	11,497
In constant 1947–49 dollars	4,099	6,355	5,970	7,084	7,660
Net national product, in current dollars (billions)	16	98	250	417	577
Ratio of total wealth to net national product	5.6	4.5	3.7	4.1	3.8

Sources: Wealth estimates are from R.W. Goldsmith, *The National Wealth of the United States in the Postwar Period*, Tables A-1 and A-2, extended to 1964 by J. W. Kendrick, assisted by A. Japha. Net national product estimates for 1929 through 1964 are based on Department of Commerce numbers with depreciation revalued to current replacement cost by J. W. Kendrick; NNP for 1900 is based on a compilation by Simon Kuznets.

Please note how the tabulation states national wealth (physical or
tangible properties) in current dollars, as well as constant (1947–
1949) dollars. This is quite helpful, because it enables one to eliminate price inflation in arriving at the real increase in national wealth.
Note the apparent increase in wealth as compared with the real
increase between different years (Table 50).

The foregoing tabulation indicates quite clearly how the sinking
purchasing power of the dollar, i.e., the increases in prices, can provide an illusory concept as to the true growth in wealth in terms of
physical properties.

TABLE 50

PERCENTAGE INCREASE IN TANGIBLE
PROPERTIES OR NATIONAL WEALTH

	Apparent Increase (in current dollars)	Actual Increase (in constant 1947– 1949 dollars)
Between 1929 and 1948	111.4%	13.5%
Between 1948 and 1958	83.5%	41.0%
Between 1958 and 1964	30.5%	19.0%
Between 1929 and 1964	406.4%	90.4%

Source: Computed from *Morgan Guaranty Survey* wealth data.

It is completely understandable that there was very little real (constant dollar) increase in physical properties between the years 1929 and 1948 because this period had consisted primarily of the Depression and the World War II years. However, equally understandable is the fact that the kiting of wages and prices immediately after the war (when the income tax was "passed on" to the consumer) had provided the illusion that tangible properties had increased 111.4 percent for the period in terms of current collars, whereas the actual real wealth increase was a mere 13.5 percent when computed in constant dollars.

In the succeeding ten years (1948 to 1958) the illusory increase was 83.5 percent; and the real increase was only 41.0 percent. Despite a considerable fanfare concerning an accelerating "Gross National Productivity," the succeeding six years (1958 to 1964) reported a mere 30.5 percent increase even on basis of using inflated dollars, and when constant dollars were employed the real increase was a paltry 19.0 percent.

Finally, for the thirty-five years elapsing between 1929 and the year 1964, the growth in wealth (physical properties) was truly depressing. Although this period included almost twenty years of postwar prosperity that had been advertised as years of great productivity and an expanding economy, American wealth, stated in constant dollars, did not even double. Of course, this shabby result lies hidden behind an illusory increase in wealth of 406.4 percent, when wealth is computed in inflationary (current) dollars!

144

Proceeding next to compare the increase in national debt with the growth in national wealth, we can, through use of simple arithmetic, compute the average annual increase in both total debt and total wealth (physical properties) for reasonably comparable spans of years. Relying upon this approach, one can decide whether an accumulation of wealth, i.e., physical properties, has at least counterbalanced the increases in national debt.

Considering the comparison first on the basis of *current* (inflating) dollar values, the figures are as follows:

TABLE 51

COMPARISON OF ANNUAL INCREASES, PHYSICAL PROPERTIES
vs. DEBT AT CURRENT DOLLARS

Earlier Period	Average annual increase in national wealth, period 1948–1958	77.5 billion dollars
	Average annual increase in total private and government debt, period 1945–1960	38.3 billion dollars
Latest Period	Average annual increase in national wealth, period 1958–1964	86.7 billion dollars
	Average annual increase in total private and government debt, period 1960–1965	82.7 billion dollars

Source: Computed from *Morgan Guaranty Survey* debt figures and wealth data.

These comparisons reveal the startling fact that the annual expansion in total debt in the first half of the 1960s was fast approaching the point of equaling the annual increase in national wealth (physical properties) as estimated, *even though existing wealth had been revalued upwards as prices had increased by estimating wealth at current dollar values.*

However, if the same comparison is made employing a constant dollar computation to eliminate price increases, the result is even more alarming. The comparison of the average annual increase in debt and in wealth, but with the real wealth estimated on basis of *1947–1949 dollars,* appears in Table 52.

Some persons may refuse to accept the comparison shown in Table

145

TABLE 52

COMPARISON OF ANNUAL INCREASES, PHYSICAL
PROPERTIES AT CONSTANT DOLLARS vs. DEBT

Earlier Period	Average annual increase in national wealth, period 1948–1958	36.1 billion dollars
	Average annual increase in total private and government debt, period 1945–1960	38.3 billion dollars
Latest Period	Average annual increase in national wealth, period 1958–1964	39.5 billion dollars
	Average annual increase in total private and government debt, period 1960–1965	82.7 billion dollars

Source: Computed from *Morgan Guaranty Survey* debt figures and wealth data.

52 that reveals an average annual increase in debt that is more than twice the increase in physical properties during the period 1960 to 1965. These persons may contend that the comparison is unfair, since the debt has been considered at *current value dollars,* whereas the properties have been taken at *constant dollars.* There is, of course, considerable validity to such contention. Nevertheless, should the government now attain success in controlling inflation, and should future price levels return to those experienced during 1947–1949, there can only be one conclusion. And the conclusion is that the average increase in debt in the early 1960s will prove to be twice the real increase in wealth (physical properties) for that period. Obviously, the dollars borrowed must be repaid no matter what the future level of prices might happen to be. And let us bear in mind, too, that in the year 1949, or thereabouts, price inflation was already well under way. Hence it is not too illogical to assume that perhaps, at some future date, price levels could return to the levels of 1947–1949, and this could happen before the total sums borrowed have been repaid.

Another method of inquiring into the economic validity of the huge increase in debt is to compute the ratio of total private and government debt to total national wealth or physical properties. Employing current (inflated) dollars that ratio recently was as follows:

TABLE 53

CURRENT DOLLAR WEALTH (PHYSICAL PROPERTIES)
vs. TOTAL DEBT

Estimated U.S. wealth in current dollars at the close of 1964	2,223 billion dollars
Private and government debt at the close of 1965	1,450.7 billion dollars
Ratio of debt to national wealth	65.3%

Source: Computed from *Morgan Guaranty Survey* debt figures and wealth data.

The foregoing reveals that debt bulks extremely large when compared with estimated national wealth. *But* note the result when estimated real national wealth is considered by employing *constant* (1947–1949) dollars for this same comparison.

TABLE 54

CONSTANT DOLLAR WEALTH (PHYSICAL PROPERTIES)
vs. TOTAL DEBT

Estimated U.S. wealth in constant (1947–1949) dollars at the close of 1964	1,481 billion dollars
Private and government debt at the close of 1965	1,450.7 billion dollars
Ratio of debt to national wealth	98%

Source: Computed from *Morgan Guaranty Survey* debt figures and wealth data.

Stated simply, any downward fluctuation that would bring prices back to 1947–1949 levels would cause the total private and government debt just about to equal the estimated national wealth (the value of accumulated physical properties).

The foregoing calls to mind the fact that in recent years a new type of borrowing procedure has been introduced under which the borrower's promise to repay is restricted to the income from, and the

147

security of, the property mortgaged, but without the borrower incurring any personal liability requiring him to repay the debt. Hence, the loan security depends entirely upon the income from the property and the continued value of the property. It is somewhat startling to note that some teachers' retirement (pension) funds have engaged in this type of loaning procedure in conjunction with multi-million-dollar mortgage loans.* That a general price decline to 1947–1949 levels could place these loans in a hazardous position is a distinct possibility.

In reviewing the figures concerning national debt and national wealth, one should remember that some economic experts find a sort of comfort in computing statistical data on a per capita basis. I do not accept that approach because it takes for granted, when applied to debt, that all persons share the wealth in the same proportions (per capita) as they are burdened with debt. Nevertheless, since per capita figures on debt and wealth have been made available, the per capita results can be the subject of comment.

Table 49 ("Wealth, People, and Product") presents wealth estimates on a per capita basis. When current (inflated) dollars are employed, the per capita wealth increased from $3,586 in 1929 to $11,-497 in 1964. However, when the real United States wealth is estimated at constant (1947–1949) dollars, the per capita wealth increased little, the per capita wealth estimate being $6,355 for 1929 and $7,660 in 1965.

Turning now to the "Gross Debt in the United States" (Table 46), when this is computed on a per capita basis, we find that the per capita debt has soared from $1,750 in 1930 to $7,500 in 1965.

Acknowledging that there is a one-year spread in each case as to the years employed for the comparison, nevertheless, if we relate the estimated per capita real national wealth computed in constant dollars to a per capita debt expressed in current dollars (the dollars at the time the debt was incurred) there is a most shocking result (Table 55).

The employment of debt and wealth figures for 1929 should not

*There could be no better evidence as to the ease with which mortgage loans could be made—of course, this was before "tight money" developed.

TABLE 55

COMPARISON CONSTANT DOLLAR WEALTH (PHYSICAL
PROPERTIES) PER CAPITA vs. TOTAL DEBT PER CAPITA

	1929 (for wealth) 1930 (for debt)	1964 (for wealth) 1965 (for debt)
Per capita national wealth expressed in constant (1947–1949) dollars	$6,355.00	$7,660.00
Per capita debt	$1,750.00	$7,500.00

be taken as an implication that American borrowing practices for
1929 should serve as an acceptable standard. In fact, two political
opponents (President Hoover and President Roosevelt) both spoke
out against the borrowing extremes of the late 1920s. Since those two
political opponents agreed on that point, one wonders what their
reaction would have been had they lived to see the condition reflected in the following tabulation:

TABLE 56

THE RATIO OF DEBT TO WEALTH

	National Wealth (physical properties) at Dollar Values in Effect for Year Considered	Total Private and Government Debt	Ratio of Debt to Wealth
1929 (wealth) 1930 (debt)	439 billion dollars	214.3 billion dollars	49.0%
1964 (wealth) 1965 (debt)	2,223 billion dollars	1,450.7 billion dollars	65.3%

Source: Computed from *Morgan Guaranty Survey* debt figures and wealth data.

It is emphasized that the foregoing comparison is stated in current
dollars, without any adjustment to the increases in national wealth
and in debt that was caused by inflation.

The facts reviewed in this chapter reveal how uncontrolled spending, coupled with a continuously inflating price structure, has led to
massive borrowing. It is more than obvious that kiting prices caused
the soaring in total national debt. In fact, in addition to the incentives

149

for borrowing provided by the Federal income tax, price increases of and by themselves provided an incentive for borrowing. Stated simply, Americans borrowed to buy with the expectation that prices in the future (when the debt had to be repaid) had to be higher. Practically everyone believed that "debt can be repaid in cheaper dollars."

Nevertheless, all of this evidence combined does not eliminate the possibility that America's nonhuman—that is, mechanical productive —plant might have been increased tremendously to compensate for the huge concentration on nonproductive spending and the curtailment in work effort. Considerable credence has been extended to the supposition that a vast improvement has been made to America's productive plant and that this has contributed greatly to America's increases in productivity that have been so broadly advertised.

In the circumstances, where we already know that economic activity has become considerably centered in government, in nonprofit enterprise, and in nonproductive work, a measurement of the increase in the American productive plant would be meaningless unless we consider the mechanical-plant increase in relation to increases in the "plant" of other forms of economic enterprise. In other words, the explanation of American productive plant must be considered relative; that is, the explanation must be measured in form of the relationship of the American productive plant to other classes of physical assets, i.e., to wealth.

By coincidence, the same August 19, 1966, issue of *The Morgan Guaranty Survey* previously referred to also included a tabulation entitled "The Forms Wealth Takes." This tabulation listed various categories of physical properties in relation to the total of all estimated American physical properties. Hence, we are able to conclude that those categories that represent the American productive plant have, in fact, increased as a proportion of total physical properties. This is shown in Table 57.

In order to compare the physical plant of productive enterprises with that of nonproductive enterprises, it is a simple matter to extricate from the tabulation those categories that have the greatest significance for the comparison. Observing that process, we extend consideration to the figures in Table 58.

150

TABLE 57

THE FORMS WEALTH TAKES
(as a % of total)

	1900	1929	1948	1964
Structures	39.8	43.2	48.4	50.2
Residential	19.8	21.8	25.2	24.7
Business	16.4	14.8	12.4	13.1
Public and other	3.5	6.6	10.7	12.4
Other Reproducibles	27.5	28.1	30.9	30.9
Producer durables	7.4	8.7	9.4	10.9
Consumer durables	7.0	9.6	9.2	11.7
Business inventories	11.3	8.7	9.3	7.4
Monetary metals	1.8	1.1	3.0	0.9
Nonreproducible assets	35.3	25.8	19.3	16.8
Agricultural land	18.4	8.7	6.4	5.7
Business land	3.6	5.2	4.2	3.9
Residential land	8.4	8.2	5.0	4.7
Public land and other	4.9	3.8	3.7	2.5
Net foreign assets	2.6	2.8	1.4	2.1
Total wealth	100.0	100.0	100.0	100.0

Source: R. W. Goldsmith and R. E. Lipsey, *Studies in the National Balance Sheet of the United States*, Volume I, Table II, extended to 1964 by J. W. Kendrick, assisted by A. Japha.

TABLE 58

	The Concentration in Public Structures			
	1900	1929	1948	1964
	(as a percentage of total wealth or physical properties)			
Structures				
Business	16.4	14.8	12.4	13.1
Public and other	3.5	6.6	10.7	12.4
Other Reproducibles				
Producer durables	7.4	8.7	9.4	10.9

Table 58 provides the conclusion that business structures reflected an almost continuous decrease as a proportion of all physical properties, except for a slight upturn in the year 1964. Public and other structures, on the other hand, reflected a continuous increase as a proportion of total physical properties. As a matter of fact, public structures as a proportion of total physical properties have almost

doubled since 1929, whereas business structures are a smaller proportion of the total than these were in 1929. Although producer
durables reflected an increase, the increase is most modest in size.

One can hardly place much faith in the possibility that the increase
in the American productive plant has been of a sufficient magnitude
to overcome the lack of production on the part of greatly increased
nonproductive enterprise. The cold fact of the matter is that in 1964
business structures and public and other structures both represented
almost identical proportions of the total national physical properties.

These figures on the make-up of physical properties simply add to
the accumulated evidence that America has in fact been converted
to a nation of nonproducers. No matter whether we examine the
GNP data, the employment statistics or the physical assets, we come
to the conclusion that America is anything but productive in areas
that produce for the support of Americans.

This is the cause of inflation that has never been explained to the
American people. This, too, is the cause of Americans going into debt
to such an extent that tight money was inevitable.

CHAPTER 10

The Effect of Boom-Bust on Economic Safeguards

As already mentioned, the same Federal Government control that began to regulate the economy in 1933 was ultimately responsible for inciting the greatest boom-bust pattern ever experienced by the American economy. Equally paradoxical, the depression-bred laws that had been intended to serve as built-in economic safeguards eventually betrayed the American people into believing that a prosperity based upon boom-bust practices could at the same time endure and be perpetual.

To explain these weird developments it is best to summarize what has been explained in preceding chapters. Americans at the close of World War II were in a highly liquid (cash) position with a minimum of debt. Psychologically, people had "learned their lesson" during the Great Depression. Americans were not about to repeat the errors of the 1920s and they really did not need the policing of the various economic control measures to guide them in their economic transactions.

Nevertheless, it should have been anticipated that conservative economic philosophies would become diluted by the strong dose of inflation that had been introduced in 1946–1947, immediately after the wage-and-price-freezing laws were removed, and when the income tax was passed on to the consumer. Equally understandable, conservative practices took another beating along about 1949 when Federal Government spending began, in obvious fashion, to inflate the economy so as to cause purchasing power (demand) to exceed available goods and services (the supply). Finally, conservative economic practices were literally swept away when the late John F. Kennedy became President. Then the smoldering economic fires were fed with the equivalent of gasoline through the "investment credit" and the "tax cut." From that time forward all lingering doubts about the boom-bust aspects of the American economy no longer had much foundation.

In this chapter, I will show how regulatory laws and conservative practices became twisted and warped to satisfy an inflationary prosperity moving upward. These laws were intended to protect Americans against the unwise economic acts of their fellows, but the laws could not perform their intended purpose under the pressure of inflationary spending by a Federal Government that could confiscate workers' incomes (through the income tax), and spend at will without disciplinary control. However, the economic control laws still remained on the statute books to serve the dubious purpose of misleading the public into believing that a completely obvious boom-bust prosperity was indeed durable and lasting because of some built-in economic safeguards.

It is relatively simple to explain how the supposed economic safeguards were rendered impotent. I shall start with the Federal Savings & Loan Associations that were provided during the depression to guard the savings of the thrifty who were unsophisticated in investment matters.

The Federal Government became involved in mutual thrift organizations because, in the early 1930s, the public's confidence in the then-existing state-chartered building and loan associations was at a low level. At that time, the holders of the shares of the state-chartered building and loans could not obtain cash for their shares because the associations could not meet the demands for repurchase of the

154

shares of quite a number of investors at the same time. Further, the demand for the repurchase of shares was arising at the very time that the associations were finding it difficult to collect the payments of interest and principal upon the mortgages in which the shareholders' funds had been invested. Needless to state, the associations could not raise additional funds through the sale of shares to other investors in an economic atmosphere lacking liquidity; furthermore, there were very few potential investors with cash to invest. Hence, those building and loan shareholders that needed cash had to sell their holdings through "grocery front" investment houses at any price the shares would bring. This proved to be a sad experience for the unsophisticated building and loan investors who had bought their shares with the expectation that they could be sold back to the association at any time to recover the cash invested, somewhat like withdrawing cash deposited in a bank.

Congress decided that a public faith in mutual thrift organizations had to be restored. Otherwise, the savings of the thrifty would not provide the funds needed for home mortgages. The solution was to provide some Federally chartered associations that were not to bear the unpopular name "building and loan." Along with the change in name, the new Federally chartered associations were specifically authorized to sell only shares to the public. Hence, these new associations were supposed to avoid any suggestion that an investment could be withdrawn "upon demand." However, the investors were given the assurance that their investments in the Federally chartered associations were "insured" up to a stated dollar amount by an instrumentality of the Federal Government.

The intent of Congress, as summarized above, was clearly reflected in the law, which read:

> Sec. (a) In order to provide local mutual thrift institutions in which people may invest their funds and in order to provide for the financing of homes, the Board is authorized, under such rules and regulations as it may prescribe, to provide for the organization, incorporation, examination, operation, and regulation of associations to be known as "Federal Savings and Loan Associations," and to issue charters therefor, giving primary consideration to the best practices of local

155

mutual thrift and home-financing institutions in the United States.

Sec. (b) Such associations shall raise their capital only in the form of payments on such shares as are authorized in their charter, which shares may be retired as is therein provided. No deposits shall be accepted and no certificates of indebtedness shall be issued except for such borrowed money as may be authorized by regulations of the Board.

12 U. S. Code 1464

Moreover, another part of the statute made it clear, too, that the new Federal Savings and Loan Associations were not intended to drive existing local thrift and home-financing organizations out of business by providing:

> No charter shall be granted except to persons of good character and responsibility, nor unless in the judgment of the Board a necessity exists for such an institution in the community to be served, nor unless there is a reasonable probability of its usefulness and success, nor unless the same can be established without undue injury to properly conducted existing local thrift and home-financing institutions.
>
> 12 U. S. Code 1464

Perhaps the reader may wonder how these plainly stated words in the law could possibly have produced the condition, now prevalent, where the Federal Savings and Loans not only represent themselves as deposit institutions but also monopolize quite a segment of the thrift and home-financing business. The answer is that for about fifteen years the Federal Home Loan Bank Board interpreted the words of Congress in a straightforward manner, but later, in 1949, the Board added a factor of sophistication to its interpretation. The manner in which this one Federal administrative agency interpreted the same law differently to adjust for changes in the economic climate is worth an examination in depth. It demonstrates the futility of expecting a law, *administered by humans,* to police economic transactions that are always affected by psychological reactions.

There can be no question that initially, and for some fifteen years after the Savings and Loan law was enacted, the Federal Home Loan Bank Board decided that these associations were to sell shares only and were not to accept deposits. The Board devised a charter for the associations (Charter K) that plainly stated:

> . . . The association shall not accept deposits from the public or issue any evidence of indebtedness except for advances. It shall not represent itself as a deposit institution.

And the Board regularly reminded the Federal Savings and Loan Associations that they were to sell shares only, and not accept deposits. For example, the *Federal Home Loan Bank Review*, Volume 1, No. 6, March 1935, mentioned how the state-chartered building and loans had gotten into difficulty by failing to distinguish between the long-term savings in those associations and the demand deposits in a commercial bank:

> . . . It has, because of public failure to differentiate the long-term savings invested in building and loan associations from demand deposits in commercial banks, aggravated withdrawal and repurchase problems. (Page 202)

This same publication then proceeded to warn the Federal Savings and Loans against misleading investors:

> Do not refer to a share account as a "savings account." Under the statute it is a share account, not a savings account. Such expressions as "interest on savings" are misleading. (Page 207)

The publication also furnished samples of advertising leaflets, all of which emphasized how a savings and loan investor was purchasing shares, with remarks such as:

> Save through Federal Savings and Loan Optional Savings Shares
> Save regularly through Federal Savings and Loan Installment Shares
>
> Invest in Federal Savings and Loan Full-Paid Income Shares
> Invest in Federal Savings and Loan Prepaid Shares

The Federal Savings and Loan Insurance Corporation, the instrumentality that insured the savings in these associations, held the same view as the Federal Home Loan Bank Board on the point that no Savings and Loan was to represent that holders of "its securities" (sic) would be paid on demand. One of the regulations of the Insurance Corporation stated:

> Demand Securities. No insured institution may issue any demand securities or advertise or represent that it will pay holders of its securities on demand.

Nevertheless, after fifteen years of adherence to the plain words of the law, the Federal Home Loan Bank Board decided to read the law differently. It was in 1949, the year that was marked by a general relaxation of the depression-bred economic restrictions, that the Board reversed its interpretation without any change in the law. From that point forward, investors in Federal Savings and Loans held "savings accounts" rather than "shares." The best way of demonstrating this about-face procedure is to supply the definitions of a Savings and Loan investment on a before and after basis, viz:

Subject Matter	Before 1949 Change	After 1949 Change
Share Capital	Paragraph 6 of Charter "K" provided—"Par. 6.—Share capital.—The share capital of the association shall consist of the aggregate of payments upon share accounts and dividends credited thereto less redemption and repurchase payments. . . . Share accounts of $100 or multiples thereof may be known as investment share accounts, consisting of full-paid income shares. All other share accounts shall be known as savings share accounts. Payments upon share accounts shall be called share payments. . . ."	Sections 141.3 and 141.4 of the Regulations provided—"Section 141.3—Capital.—The term 'capital' means the aggregate of the payments on *savings accounts* in a Federal association, plus earnings credited thereto, less lawful deductions therefrom. "Section 141.4—Savings Account—The term '*savings account*' means the monetary interest of the holder thereof in the capital of a Federal association and consists of the withdrawal value of such interest."

It should have been self-evident that as soon as Saving and Loans stopped selling shares and obtained their capital through investments in "savings accounts," they were converted into deposit institutions. How else could an investment in a savings account be described? Nor could there be any question that public investors considered amounts placed in a "savings account" as subject to immediate withdrawal at any time. This was acknowledged by the General Manager of the Federal Savings & Loan Insurance Corporation in a public address when he said:

> Quite generally, savings and loan associations have created the impression that they fully expect to pay withdrawals on demand. Often outright written or oral statements are made to this effect, and, even more frequently, there is reliance upon tacit understanding. . . .

> Viewed strictly in this light, there can be little doubt about the need for reasonable liquidity if associations are to live up to their obligations to the saving public. The alternative, of course, is to advertise the rights of associations to prorate funds in the event of emergency. However, when the cold realities of this policy are considered, it must be clear that its effect would probably be detrimental to the best interests of the savings and loan business. . . .

> (Taken from Public Address by Dr. William H. Husband, reported in the letter of the Federal Home Loan Bank of Greensboro, North Carolina, Volume V, No. 1, issued under date of March 31, 1956.)

Of course, Dr. Husband was accurate in advocating a "reasonable liquidity" for these associations if they were to be in position to meet their obligations to the public. However, he did not explain how that liquidity could be attained if the funds of these associations were for the most part invested in long-term mortgages.

One could say, too, that Dr. Husband employed a poor choice of language in referring to any publicity concerning the proration of funds in case of an emergency as *advertising*. But even more serious was his comment that a release of facts to the public would probably be detrimental to the best interests of the savings and loan business. Was Dr. Husband assuming that legal obligations to investors were to be ignored whenever they might adversely affect the success of an investment project? Certainly such an attitude was completely contrary to the purposes of the Securities & Exchange Act as these were applied to the issuance of shares by other corporations.

Some Wisconsin bankers decided that the change in regulations by the Federal Home Loan Bank Board placed the Federal Savings and Loans in the business of accepting deposits, and this was illegal since only banks could accept deposits. Accordingly, the legality of the change in regulations was challenged in *Wisconsin Bankers Association, et al, v. Albert J. Robertson, et al, comprising the Federal Home Loan Bank Board.* * However, both the Federal District Court of the District of Columbia, and the Court of Appeals for the District of Columbia, upheld the validity of the challenged Savings and Loan regulations. The Appeals Court's opinion in part commented on the matter of the change from "shares" to "savings accounts" as follows:

> The section of the 1949 regulations which defines capital in terms of payments on savings accounts is immediately followed by a section which defines the term "savings account" as "the monetary interest of the holder thereof in the capital of a Federal association and consists of the withdrawal value of such interest." It seems quite clear, therefore, that the words "savings accounts" in the regulation defining "capital" have the same meaning as the word "shares" in the statutory provision governing the raising of capital.

However, in a concurring opinion Circuit Judge Burger** included the following observation:

> I concur fully with Chief Judge Miller's opinion. The essence of appellant's claim is that under the challenged regulations federal savings associations are permitted to look and act more and more like banks and should be deemed therefore to be engaged illegally in banking business. I am constrained to concede that these associations are indeed coming to be regarded by the public much as the equivalent of a bank. For a great number of people they are a substitute for a bank and in that sense compete directly with banks. But Congress was and is well aware of these factors.***

*The author was the attorney for the plaintiffs that were challenging the Savings and Loan regulations.
**Now Chief Justice Burger of the United States Supreme Court.
***Congress, however, did not demonstrate its awareness until about seven years later, in 1968. At least in 1968 Congress enacted a statute that enabled Savings

That the payment may be regarded by the customer as a "deposit" or even called at times a deposit by the association does not make it a legal counterpart of a deposit in a bank. The "depositor" in a federal association is not a creditor as is the depositor in a bank. . . .

These words expressed by a Federal court prompt an interesting question. How can the Federal Government on the one hand demand that security investors be given all of the facts concerning publicly held corporations, but on the other hand permit a Federal agency to operate in a way that could cause the unsophisticated thrifty who place their savings in a savings and loan possibly to confuse their share investment with a bank deposit? As the Honorable Mr. Justice Burger had noted, "Congress was and is well aware of these factors." However, when Congress, by a change in law in 1968, legalized the process of savings and loans accepting "savings deposits," was Congress expecting the public to understand what Judge Burger had said—that calling a savings and loan investment a deposit "does not make it a legal counterpart of a deposit in a bank"?

No matter what the public understood, the public in fact regarded savings and loans as equivalent to banks, as shown by increased savings and loan investments compared with increased time deposits in commercial banks after the 1949 change (Table 59).

But why should the public be concerned on point of whether the savings and loans accept deposits or sell shares? Is it not the case that no matter how an investment in a savings and loan may be legally described, the investment is insured? Yes, savings and loan investments are insured up to a stated amount by the Federal Savings and Loan Insurance Corporation, a Federal corporation whose assets and borrowing capacity furnish the security behind the insurance of savings and loan investments. Somewhat similarly, the Federal Deposit Insurance Corporation is another Federal corporation whose assets and borrowing capacity furnish the security behind the insurance of bank deposits.

and Loans to "raise capital in the form of such savings deposits, shares, or other accounts. . . ." This was like a "shotgun marriage," since the change in law provided statutory legality for what the Savings and Loans had been doing for something like nineteen years without benefit of any statute.

TABLE 59

BANK TIME DEPOSITS vs.
SAVINGS AND LOAN SAVINGS ACCOUNTS

| December | Stated in Billions of Dollars | |
	Commercial Banks Time Deposits*	Savings and Loans Capital**
1929	19.9	6.237
1938	26.4	4.077
1947	35.4	9.8
1948	36.0	11.0
1949	36.4	12.5
1950	36.7	14.0
1951	38.3	16.1
1952	41.2	19.2
1953	44.6	22.8
1954	48.4	27.3
1955	50.2	32.1
1956	52.1	37.1
1957	57.5	41.9
1958	65.5	48.0
1959	67.4	54.6
1960	72.7	62.1
1961	82.5	70.9
1962	97.5	80.4
1963	110.8	91.3

Sources of Information: *Federal Reserve.
**Federal Savings and Loan Insurance Corporation.

However, these two Federally established insurance corporations seem to differ in expressing an opinion as to the adequacy of their assets in insuring deposits, or share investments, as the case may be.

For example, the Federal Deposit Insurance Corporation, in its annual report for the year ended December 31, 1955, expressed a rather reserved opinion about the future adequacy of the insurance of bank deposits. This took the form of a footnote to the June 30, 1955, financial statement of the F.D.I.C., which read:

At June 30, 1955, the deposit insurance fund was equivalent to 1.42 percent of the insured deposits in all banks, estimated by the Corporation at 112.2 billion dollars. This fund, however, is not a measure of the deposit insurance risk, and *its adequacy to meet future losses will depend on future economic conditions* which cannot be predicted.

162

Based on data compiled by the Corporation, the fund appears to be adequate to cover any potential losses at June 30, 1955. (Italics added.)

A somewhat contrary viewpoint, almost belligerently stated, was expressed by the Federal Savings and Loan Insurance Corporation on the matter of the insurance on share accounts (and/or deposits) in savings and loans, viz:

THE INSURANCE CONCEPT

There is no magic in insurance, but rather it puts into effect a time-honored principle—"In unity, there is strength." Through the premiums paid by the insured members and the earnings realized on the invested assets, a common central fund is created that may be diverted to any point of weakness. In other words, the combined force of many may be brought into action the instant that trouble develops in any single institution or in any particular area. When, in this manner, difficulties are stopped at the source, the familiar spreading of weakness that was so much in evidence in the past is forestalled. The plugging of the leak saves the dike.

Of course, those who yield to imaginary fears raise the question of what would happen if every insured institution should encounter serious difficulty at the same time. Or, the dire thought is raised that all savers might want their money at once. There is but one answer—such eventualities are impossible, for if they were conceivable, there would be no funds available to conduct economic activity in any form. Even so, protective facilities, discussed in detail later, are available to meet emergency conditions and, in fact, serve to prevent them through the confidence and unified strength generated by insurance.

Over the years the American public has become fully aware of the advantages of insurance of savings and now regards such protection as an essential part of the nation's financial structure.

("20th Anniversary Report, 1934–1954," Federal Savings and Loan Insurance Corporation, Washington, D.C.)

However, in spite of the rather arrogantly expressed assurances of the Federal Savings and Loan Insurance Corporation, still another arm of the Federal Government, the Internal Revenue Service, has permitted commercial banks to assume that banks in the future may once again experience the serious bad-debt losses they experienced during the Great Depression. This concerns the bad-debt reserve procedure extended to commercial banks that was described as follows in a U. S. Treasury Department Report, dated July 14, 1961, and submitted to the House Ways and Means Committee:

> Most taxable institutions, in establishing bad-debt reserves for Federal income tax purposes, are not permitted to base their anticipated loss experience upon the experience of the economic collapse of the 1930s. However, because of considerations peculiar to certain financial institutions, *the commercial banks are permitted to establish bad-debt reserves equal to three times their average loss experience for the worst 20-consecutive-year period beginning after 1927. This formula, therefore, does take into account depression experience.* . . . (Italics added.)

Obviously, the opinions of the three Federal Agencies mentioned differ broadly concerning the factor of risk in the future of financial affairs. And the Chief Justice of the United States Supreme Court, Warren Burger, while on the bench of the U. S. Court of Appeals for the District of Columbia had plainly said: "The 'depositor' in a federal association is not a creditor as is the depositor in a bank." Meanwhile, however, the Federal Savings and Loan Associations have continued blandly to attract the savings of the thrifty with advertising that does not even define the legal character of a savings and loan investment.

Life insurance policies are another form of built-in economic safeguard. Life insurance is an investment for the funds of the thrifty who want to avoid risk and speculation. Insurance has been broadly advertised as a medium for saving independent of the insurance coverage a policy provides. It is quite interesting to note that the economic conditions in 1949 that had prompted the Federal Home Loan Bank Board to change the name of a savings and loan investment also caused life insurance companies to discard conservative investment procedures.

For example, the 1949 annual report issued by one particular life insurance company to its policyholders complained about the low interest return on U. S. Government and corporate bonds:

> Interest rates on new investments during the first six months of 1949 continued at about the same level as 1948, but the trend since the middle of the year has been downward. At the end of the year, interest yields on U. S. Government and corporate bonds were lower than at any time since early 1946. The fiscal policies of the Federal Government continue to result in low interest rates and thus produce a relatively unsatisfactory return on the savings of thrifty and provident citizens. It is regrettable that the dollars saved and productively put to work do not receive more adequate wages.

However, almost twenty years later, this same insurance company, in a September 1969 report to its field agents, proudly commented about the high return on its common stock investments:

> ... Over the last 10 year period, the common stock account has earned 12 percent, including dividends and both realized and unrealized capital gains. . . .

This report to the field agents emphasized that the insurance company's stock investments had not approached the legal limit:

> ... We are allowed by law to hold 15 percent of assets in common stocks and preferred stocks. We currently are at about the 5 percent level for common stock, or an account of approximately $270 million (as of May 31).

However, the report went on to explain how the insurance company could obtain speculative profits through the mortgage loan route:

> ... At the present time, because of market conditions, about 30 percent of our mortgages carry incentive equities in the form of participation in the gross income stream, participation in land sales, profits, warrants, options on stock and other devices. . . .

One need not be too worldly-wise in investment matters to know that a mortgage with an "incentive equity" represented the case

165

where the borrower consented to the lender participating in the profits from the borrower's business so that the borrower could obtain a mortgage loan under conditions not otherwise obtainable. Hence, one can assume that the insurance company had decided to sacrifice either a factor of security or a higher interest return in making its mortgage investments, in order to obtain the "incentive equity."

There could be little question but that this insurance company had changed its investment policies between 1949 and 1969 in order to obtain an increased annual return on its investments. And this change in policy is clearly revealed when one compares the percentage distribution of its investments by categories as they are given in this insurance company's annual reports between the years 1929 and 1968:

TABLE 60

A LIFE INSURANCE COMPANY
DISTRIBUTION OF INVESTMENTS BY PERCENT OF TOTAL

	1929	1939	1949	1959	1968
Bonds	33.35%	55.40%	76.36%	53.20%	39.70%
Preferred Stock			1.98%	0.80%	3.46%
Common Stock				1.40%	4.64%
Mortgage Loans	44.62%	23.49%	13.55%	34.10%	34.30%
Real Estate	0.61%	4.20%	1.79%	2.60%	4.00%
Policy Loans	17.51%	13.17%	3.60%	4.70%	11.30%*
Other Investments	3.91%	3.74%	2.72%	3.20%	2.60%
Total	100.00%	100.00%	100.00%	100.00%	100.00%

*The 1970 annual report of this insurance company reported policy loans at 16.8% of all investments, thus bringing this ratio directly in line with the position it had in 1929.

The foregoing tabulation plainly reveals how one insurance company had converted its investments to attain a highly liquid position (an emphasis upon bond investments) during the twenty-year interval between 1929 and 1949, when bond investments were increased and mortgage loans decreased. In fact, one could assume that the high concentration in bond investments in 1949 was the direct cause for the complaint about low interest rates as quoted from the company's 1949 Annual Report.

But after 1949 the insurance company switched its investments back into mortgages, stocks and real estate, and bondholdings were reduced. In fact, the percentage invested in different categories by this insurance company for 1968 was substantially similar to the distribution for 1929, and entirely different from that for the year 1949. Hence, even as the Federal Home Loan Bank Board had found it expedient, in 1949, to discard the frank acknowledgment that investors in savings and loans were purchasing shares, this insurance company at about the same time decided to discard more conservative investment practices to obtain a higher return on its investments.

As a matter of fact, the changes in investment policy adopted by this insurance company reflected generally the practices of all American life insurance companies. This is revealed in the following tabulation:

TABLE 61

ASSET CLASSIFICATIONS—
PERCENT OF TOTAL ASSETS HELD BY
UNITED STATES LIFE INSURANCE COMPANIES

	U.S. Government and Other Government Securities	Securities of Business and Industry	Mortgages	Real Estate	Policy Loans
1929	8.15%	28.6%	41.8%	2.6%	13.6%
1939	26.60%	29.2%	19.4%	7.3%	11.1%
1945	50.30%	24.7%	14.8%	1.9%	4.4%
1955	12.90%	43.9%	32.6%	2.9%	3.6%
1965	7.22%	42.7%	37.8%	3.0%	4.8%

Source: Computed from statistics published by the Institute of Life Insurance.

Even the commercial banks had to discard the condition of liquidity that had developed after the Great Depression and during World War II. Otherwise the banks could not hope to operate profitably during an inflation-inspired economy. Like the investments of this nation's insurance companies, the investment funds of commercial banks had become highly concentrated after the close of World War

II in low-interest-yielding U. S. Government bonds that were the equivalent of cash. In 1945, commercial banks as a group had government bonds equal to 94.6 percent of total deposits.

However, thereafter the government bond holdings of banks decreased and the loans made to other borrowers increased, as the following tabulation reveals:

TABLE 62

	All Commercial Banks	
Year	% of Cash plus U.S. Governments to Deposits	% of Loans to Deposits
1929	36.0%	79.0%
1939	81.0%	35.9%
1945	94.6%	19.0%
1955	62.0%	47.1%
1965	38.5%	64.4%
1970	37.4%	75.4%

Source: Ratios computed from Federal Reserve data.
(Note: Excluding interbank deposits, but including U. S. Government deposits.)

The changes in the cash and loan position of commercial banks reveals, once again, a switch to conservatism after the 1929 financial holocaust, but this was followed in turn by conditions closely approximating those in 1929 as the inflation-inspired economy prompted a discard of conservative practices.

Of course, commercial banks have been under the control of government regulations that developed out of the Great Depression. Nevertheless, this did not prevent banks from devising new and different ways for obtaining cash. One route has been for a bank to sell to the public a multi-million-dollar long-term debenture issue. Another method to obtain cash has consisted of the banks issuing "certificates of deposit" for a stated period of time. These new methods for obtaining cash should be construed as nothing more than an open acknowledgment by the banks that the funds they needed for loans to borrowers could no longer be obtained by relying only upon the traditional time- and demand-deposit sources.

It needs to be emphasized, however, that the sale of debentures and the issuance of certificates of deposit by banks was not a completely voluntary action on their part. These new procedures for obtaining money merely attested to the condition that banks had to pay interest on funds obtained for lending purposes, because the non-interest-bearing demand (checking account) deposits were not being maintained in sufficient volume.

For example, the facts show that the total demand deposits of all commercial banks increased by $66.4 billion in the short interval of time between the close of 1939 and the close of 1945. However, thereafter and during the entire succeeding twenty-year interval between the close of 1945 and the close of 1965 the increase in total demand deposits of commercial banks was only $69.4 billion *despite the national prosperity that prevailed throughout this long period.*

Hence, since commercial banks could no longer obtain sufficient funds from demand-deposit sources, the banks had been forced to attract time deposits, including certificates of deposit, by paying interest on these. This procedure caused a complete change in the relationship of the demand deposits to time deposits as the following tabulation reveals:

TABLE 63

ALL COMMERCIAL BANKS

Year	Demand Deposits	Time Deposits	Ratio of Demand to Time Deposits
	(billions of dollars)		
1929	25.5	19.9	128%
1939	30.5	15.2	201%
1945	96.9	27.2	356%
1955	126.9	48.7	260%
1965	166.3	146.7	113%
1970	186.7	229.1	82%

Source: Ratio computed from Federal Reserve data.
(Note: Excluding interbank deposits, but including U.S. Government deposits with demand deposits).

169

Once again a comparison of financial statistics reveals that by the year 1965 (just before tight money) the ratio of demand to time deposits of commercial banks closely approximated that of 1929. I need not venture an opinion as to whether this development denoted a serious erosion of the conservative conditions required in the banking business. Instead, I need merely quote from an article entitled "Bank Liquidity Reexamined," published in *Business Conditions*, a review by the Federal Reserve Bank of Chicago, for July 1966, which included the following paragraph:

> The very substantial change that has occurred in the composition of deposits in recent years also has an important bearing on the need for liquidity. Historically, time deposits have shown much greater stability over short periods (although they have undergone very wide swings secularly) than have demand deposits. Because of the rapid growth in time and savings balances during the past six years, many banks may feel comfortable with relatively small holdings of liquid assets. Whether total deposits are actually more stable, given the large volume of time and savings deposits and the greater importance of fixed maturity certificates as a component of such deposits is not entirely clear.

Even as the Federal Home Loan Bank Board, the insurance companies and the commercial banks were forced to dilute depression-bred conservative practices (the so-called "economic safeguards") under the pressures of an inflation-inspired economy, the American public had to undertake some changes, too, in the safeguards the public could ordinarily employ for future economic survival. Perhaps the most reliable safeguard for the protection of one's family security is a life insurance policy. Ordinarily, the person insured pays premiums that are accumulated by the insurance company into a reserve, and the longer the insured lives the greater the reserve to enable the insurance company to pay the "death benefit" that can contribute to the support of the family that survives the insured at the time of his death. Further, should the insured attain old age, the accumulated reserve can be taken by him as a form of retirement income.

Now it stands to reason that, under the condition of each American

170

having a large part of his earnings taken for the Federal income tax and another large part of his earnings needed to pay ever-mounting living costs, quite a number of Americans could no longer afford to pay the insurance premiums on any form of life insurance that accumulated a reserve. Confronted with these financial predicaments many Americans turned to "group insurance."

This form of insurance can be explained quite simply. It consists of a group of individuals promising one another to contribute toward the death benefit payable in the event that any member of the group should die. The premium cost of this form of insurance is very low, since there are no reserves accumulated for the future, and hence the premium cost need only cover the amounts paid to the family of a deceased member, plus the costs of the insurance administration.

However, there is a vast difference between ordinary life insurance and group insurance. Ordinary life insurance is a contract for life, continuing as long as the premiums are paid. In fact, if premium payments are discontinued, the insured is repaid the cash surrender value. Group insurance, on the other hand, continues only so long as the group continues to be insured, or so long as the insured is a member of the group. As a matter of fact, the death benefits paid because of the death of any members of a group ordinarily represent a minor fraction of the total number of persons insured. Further, the low cost of group insurance is highly illusory, because unless young persons (with a long life expectancy) are continuously added to the group, the cost of group insurance would literally skyrocket, i.e., the group insured would grow older each year, thus increasing the probability of death benefits being required to be paid.

Nevertheless, group insurance does furnish a factor of security to the family of the insured who happens to die while a member of the group. For example, should an employee be covered by group insurance, *and die while in employment,* his family would be paid.

Table 64 reveals the relationship of group insurance coverage to the total of all life insurance coverage.

These figures reveal that 45 percent of the increase in national life insurance coverage for the period from 1945 (after the close of World War II) until the year 1970 was in the form of group insurance. This

171

TABLE 64

LIFE INSURANCE COVERAGE—
RELATIONSHIP OF GROUP INSURANCE TO TOTAL
(SELECTED YEARS)
(in billions of dollars)

Years	Total of Ordinary Life, Industrial and Group Insurance	Group Insurance	% of Group Insurance to Total
1929	102.029	8.994	8.8%
1939	111.262	13.641	12.3%
1945	151.397	22.172	14.6%
1955	357.582	101.300	28.3%
1965	843.561	306.113	36.3%
1970	1,314.833	545.092	41.5%

Source: Institute of Life Insurance.

reveals how personal budgets that were burdened with income taxes and inflationary price increases could not also pay the premiums on a more permanent form of insurance.*

One more fact should be stressed concerning the increase in group insurance. For the most part, group insurance has been made available by employers to their employees, and any cost the employer might incur has had to be loaded into the cost of goods and services. Hence, the cost of insuring the lives of employees has become just another element causing the prices that the American consumer must pay to soar.

Once again this is due to the fact that American workers have had to bear an income tax burden plus higher living costs, and the workers have been unable to afford to pay the premiums on a more durable form of life insurance. Hence, one should conclude that an economic safeguard formerly available in the form of permanent insurance carried and paid for by the workers has been eliminated, although this could have served as a most reliable form of a built-in economic stabilizer.

What has been said about group life insurance applies equally to

*This conclusion applies as well to high-salaried and heavily taxed executives. The insurance provided by employers for these executives would (like group insurance) account for a large segment of the total life insurance in force.

172

hospitalization insurance. This "insurance" is nothing more than a procedure where members of a group agree to pay the cost incurred by one another for hospitalization care. As in the case of group insurance, the coverage is available only so long as the group continues, and so long as a particular insured person continues as a member of the group. At the risk of overdoing repetition, it can be stressed that the American worker, burdened as he has been with the income tax and high living costs, could not afford to pay his hospitalization costs. In fact, the cost of hospitalization insurance is generally borne, in part at least, by the employers of the workers. And, of course, this cost like many others has become a cost of products and services to be loaded into the high prices that the consumer has had to pay.

As a matter of fact, hospitalization insurance might be said to be self-defeating in that it prompts an unrestricted use of costly hospital facilities. This is best demonstrated by the manner in which the cost of hospital care has increased far beyond any increase in the Consumer Price Index:

TABLE 65

CONSUMER PRICE INDEX AND
HOSPITAL COST INDEX
(1967 = 100)

	1965	1966	1967	1968	1969	1970
Consumer Price Index (all items)	94.5	97.2	100.0	104.2	109.8	116.3
Hospital Cost Index	76.6	84.0	100.0	113.2	127.9	143.9

Obviously, like group insurance the cost of hospitalization insurance must skyrocket when the members of an insured group attain the older age plateau that makes the need for hospital care more definite and certain. This factor, coupled with the fact that insurance coverage is generally terminated when employment terminates at time of retirement, has prompted the introduction of Federal hospitalization insurance. And the costs of this Federal program were loaded upon the American taxpayers, to place even greater tax and inflated-price burdens upon the American workers.

173

What has been said about group insurance and hospitalization insurance applies for the most part to the other so-called safeguards introduced during the Great Depression. These include Social Security benefits and unemployment insurance. Time and again, Social Security benefits have had to be increased as prices have spiraled upwards. And unemployment insurance could never support any material quantity of unemployment should any large-scale American economic adversity occur.

Still another form of economic safeguard is the retirement pay programs financed by employers. Although such programs were in existence for quite a number of years for an isolated group of large employers, they became universally applicable about 1942. In that year, when Congress perceptibly increased the income tax burdens of workers, Congress also introduced into the income tax law a universally applicable program for employee retirement-pay-benefit plans. There could have been no more specific acknowledgment by Congress that the American worker could no longer pay the cost of government and at the same time save funds to provide for his own retirement.

Initially, the employee trust funds intended for retirement pay were invested in high-grade securities, generally U. S. Government bonds. However, the more prices increased because of government spending, the more futile it was to expect fixed-dollar, low-income-return government bonds to meet the eventual cost of retirement pay. And these funds have more recently been invested in common stocks and other inflation hedges in a vain effort to accumulate a fund sufficient to assure retirement pay. The risk of loss of these employee retirement funds would be tremendous should a repetition of the 1929 security-price collapse ever take place.

Incidentally, no one has bothered to tell the American worker that the more employer retirement-pay programs that are placed in operation, the greater the number of persons needed to administer these programs, which will impede still more the productivity of this nation. The foregoing observation confirms that vast numbers of Americans are engaged in nothing more productive than to administer employer retirement-pay programs in one way

174

or another.* *Of course, this administration cost has had to be loaded upon the consumer together with the funds set aside for retirement pay, and prices have climbed still higher.*

Meanwhile, the American worker was deluded into believing that he was required to save little out of the pay that remained after income taxes and after paying his high support expenses, because his support during retirement had been provided for through Social Security and/or his employer's retirement pay program. That this, too, caused a discarding of one of the most reliable of all possible economic safeguards, the responsibility of the individual to spend sparingly so as to save the utmost for his future needs, should have been completely obvious.

Finally, this review of the built-in economic safeguards turns to the depression-bred laws intended to provide investment safety for the more sophisticated investors, that is, those who place their investment funds in the bonds and stocks of publicly owned corporations. To protect these investors the Securities Act and the Securities Exchange Act had been enacted during the Great Depression. Primarily, these laws required that publicly owned corporations make full disclosures concerning their financial affairs, and required, too, that brokers and dealers in securities observe strict standards in dealing with customers. Generally speaking, the securities business was placed under the supervision of the Securities and Exchange Commission.

The securities control laws had been conceived in a hurry by theorists at the start of the depression when the Congressional hearing rooms in Washington served as a sort of guillotine where the characters of persons prominent in securities dealings could be lopped off. In those early days of the depression it was taken for granted that practically every investment loss had been caused by fraud, manipulation, profiting by insiders, inadequate margins, insufficient information to investors, and dishonest brokers. The securities laws were enacted to terminate these evils.

However, had Congress waited a few more years to allow heads to

*Some life insurance salesmen have found that the commissions on policies related to employee retirement plans furnished an easy route to wealth.

175

cool and facts to be accumulated, Congress should have noted that the great bulk of the losses of investors had not been the result of fraud or dishonesty. The actual major causes of the investment losses following the 1929 crash were (1) many corporations had neither the financial resources nor the minimum earning capacity necessary to withstand depression conditions, (2) far too many persons had been speculating in securities in the late 1920s without having either the funds or the financial understanding needed for intelligent investment, and (3) the need for cash that developed after the start of the depression had forced security holders to dump their holdings at whatever price these would bring in order to obtain much-needed cash, and this caused security prices to collapse. As a matter of fact, marketable securities could most readily be converted into cash (at a low price, of course), whereas other investments, such as real estate holdings, were literally frozen and could not readily be sold, not even at a deflated price.

None of the Federal securities laws were structured to prevent a repetition of these itemized major causes of the 1929–1932 security losses should a serious economic upheaval take place. As a matter of fact, the huge public offerings of shares in new and untried ventures in the late 1960s should strongly suggest that, despite the security laws, a condition where the public could suffer substantial investment losses could readily be repeated. Incidentally, one could suspect that the image of investor safety provided by the securities laws under the policing by the Securities and Exchange Commission has caused current-day investors to employ less care in making investments than was employed by their predecessors in the late 1920s.*

Moreover, there are persons with an understanding about the securities business who insist that the Federal regulatory authorities have not rendered security purchasing less hazardous. For example, in an article in *Barron's* weekly of May 4, 1970, entitled "End of the 'Game,'" an opinion was expressed concerning the merit of the operations of the Securities and Exchange Commission. Commenting about the Commission, the article stated:

*And, as we shall learn in a later chapter, the Federal income tax law had caused the prices of common stocks to be artificial and "rigged."

... While busy flexing its regulatory muscle all over the Street, the agency showed an astonishing willingness to ignore, in connection with the registration and sale of securities, accounting practices which have proven at best misleading and at worst tantamount to fraud.

And the article quoted a 1964 comment of George J. Stigler, the Charles R. Walgreen Distinguished Service Professor of American Institutions (Graduate School of Business, University of Chicago), who flatly stated that if one includes the cost of regulation,

grave doubts exist . . . whether the SEC has saved the purchasers of new issues one dollar.

But even more serious is the distinct possibility that major American corporations could not withstand the bloodbath of a depression as they had been able to do in the 1930s. In some instances, the financial condition of publicly owned corporations does not remotely resemble the condition of financial strength these same corporations had displayed in 1929. Here are some examples as to how seriously corporate liquidity has deteriorated because of inflationary conditions, supplemented by the fact that the income tax law has encouraged borrowing, since interest on debt is tax-deductible:

TABLE 66

CORPORATE LIQUIDITY
1929 vs. 1965 and 1967

	Ratio of Cash plus Cash Equivalent to Current Liabilities plus Long-Term Debts		
Corporate Identification	1929	1965	1967
Chemical Producer	8.48	0.03	0.13
Motor Manufacturer	4.72	0.20	0.11
Office Equipment Manufacturer	3.61	0.07	0.05
Another Motor Manufacturer	0.56	0.39	0.31
Another Chemical Producer	1.53	1.34	0.61
Department Store Chain	0.73	0.22	0.20
Foods Supplier	0.89	0.24	0.34
Another Motor Manufacturer	1.08	0.56	0.57
Another Department Store Chain	1.20	0.26	0.18

Mail Order House	3.23	0.08	0.04
Tobacco Firm	1.85	0.08	0.08
Oil Company	2.27	0.16	0.17
Another Chemical Producer	2.41	0.35	0.17
Steel Corporation	0.77	0.49	0.19
Diversified Auto Parts	1.97	0.14	0.13

Source: Computed on the basis of balance-sheet data contained in *Moody's Industrial Manuals* for applicable years.

This chapter outlines the paradox that the laws and the conservative procedures originally intended to stabilize and safeguard the economy could not withstand the onslaught of Federal Government inflationary spending and the economic abnormalities that this spending and the Federal income tax had introduced. Coupled with this is the other paradox that a public faith in supposed built-in economic safeguards has provided little more than a delusion of future economic stability for an unsuspecting public.

CHAPTER 11

The Delusion about "Inflation Hedges"

Those Americans that were worldly-wise about economic affairs
knew that continuous Federal Government spending must eventually lead to rampant price inflation. They were not about to accept
the propaganda that the American economy was soundly based, or
that America was increasing productivity so that the economy could
tolerate this spending without the demand for goods continuously
exceeding the supply, thus making everything more expensive.

These Americans reasoned that to protect their economic future
they had to invest in things that would go up in value as the price
level increased. Hence, they expected that, at any given point of
time in the future, the increase in the value of their investments
would counterbalance the price increases, and they should be able
to finance the ever-increasing costs of their future budgetary needs.
This procedure of trying to survive economically under the constant
pressure of increasing prices was known as acquiring "inflation
hedges."

There is nothing new or novel about that procedure. There was a
story, possibly apocryphal, that described how "inflation hedges"
enabled a German citizen to survive the German inflation that followed World War I. According to the story, this particular German

had anticipated the post-World War I German inflation and he loaded his basement with hog-bristle toothbrushes. When the expected inflation arrived, he sold his toothbrushes from time to time, as the occasion would demand, to provide him with funds for his skyrocketing personal living costs. The toothbrushes were an item of necessity; they increased in price with inflation and they were rather easy to sell. This particular German, so the story goes, was able to meet his budget problems during inflation.

However, had quite a number of Germans decided to hoard hog-bristle toothbrushes, causing an artificial shortage of supply that, in turn, would have prompted the price of toothbrushes to skyrocket, then the story about an alleged inflation hedge in post-World War I Germany would have had an unhappy ending for the hoarders of toothbrushes. Obviously, any frenzied buying and hoarding of toothbrushes would have made the German inflation more serious, and those buying toothbrushes could only have incurred losses. Those who had been striving to acquire inflation hedges would have been defeating the very purpose behind their hedging procedure, i.e., their own actions would have been helping to spur the inflation they were trying to hedge against.

Of course, those Americans that have been acquiring inflation hedges have not been buying hog-bristle toothbrushes as in the German story. Today, an inflation hedge must be something that cannot readily be reproduced (man-made). Anything that is man-made can be manufactured to meet the demand and, without a shortage of the intended hedge against inflation, its value cannot move upward with general price increases. The best examples of the inflation hedges sought by Americans are common stocks, real estate, paintings, art objects, antiques and similar tangible or intangible goods that are not readily capable of reproduction.

No matter how modern-day experts in the field of investment and banking may emphasize the need for acquiring inflation hedges to protect the purchasing power of an investor's savings, the acquisition of any inflation hedge should be classed as a sheer gamble rather than an investment. The person who acquires an inflation hedge is gambling (1) that general price levels will continue to increase ad infinitum; (2) that the value of his particular inflation hedge will keep pace with general price increases; and (3) that at some appropriate time in the future he will be able to sell his inflation hedge.

On the other hand, an investor should have these objectives: (1) an income return for the use of his money, and (2) a possible appreciation in the value of the investment identified with the success of the particular venture in which he has made an investment. Of course, inflation, i.e., an increase in general price levels, could also cause an investor's funds to appreciate in value, but such appreciation is apt to have little connection with the individual success of the enterprise in which the investment is made. Bear in mind, however, that the investor can get the income return and the appreciation in value of his investment that he anticipates without there being continued inflationary price increases. Contrariwise, the acquirer of an inflation hedge cannot really attain his objective of having the value of his hedge move upward unless there is an increase in the general price level.

Undoubtedly, the greatest risk that is involved in the acquisition of inflation hedges consists of the possibility of becoming crowd motivated and of buying hedges on a promiscuous basis under the supposition that the price of any hedge will go up in the future. This would be like being caught in the crowd psychology prevalent in the 1920s, a procedure sharply criticized by Bernard Baruch as quoted earlier. Promiscuous buying is not apt to result in buying hedges at the right price, nor is it conducive to selling hedges at the right time.

However, those Americans that have bought inflation hedges during the past twenty years have incurred another risk. They have been competing in buying common-stock hedges in an artificial market in which the prices for the common stocks were "rigged." This was so because: (1) the demand for common stocks was artificially kited; (2) the supply of common stocks was artificially reduced; and (3) a large number of the common-stock purchasers had practically the purchasing power of a monopolistic organization. Each of these conditions that increased the risk for the purchaser of common stocks shall be explained.

Considering first the artificial demand for inflation hedges, this was

181

caused by the Federal income tax extending a tax preference to gains from the sale of capital assets. This tax advantage did not apply to investment income in the form of interest or dividends, but only to gains from the sale of capital assets such as real estate, common stocks, art objects, etc. That this encouraged a speculation for sharp price increases over an investment for income and gradual price increases should have been taken for granted, since the greater the degree of speculation involved in any common-stock purchase, the greater the possibility of the appreciation in value that produces a low-taxed capital gain.

Now, of course, to obtain a low-taxed long-term capital gain the asset had to be held over a long term. However, at the very time (in 1942) that Congress changed the income tax law so as to tax the income of the workers with greater certainty, Congress also changed the law to shorten the "long-term" capital gain holding period. That Congress, by its action, discouraged the earning of income by working or the income from investments, while at the same time encouraging the obtaining of gains from speculation in common stocks and other inflation hedges, was obvious. In fact, if we go back to the changes in the income tax law that occurred during the Great Depression, the tax favoritism provided for speculators becomes even more obvious, viz:

TABLE 67

Year	The Tax Burden for the Worker Surtax Exemption: Husband and Wife	Minimum and Maximum Income Tax Rate	Tax Relief for the Speculator Holding Period Required to Obtain Maximum Capital Gain Tax Benefits
1936	$6,500.00	8% to 79%*	More than 10 years
1938	$6,500.00	8% to 79%*	More than 24 months
1942	$1,200.00	11% to 86%**	More than 6 months

*Combining normal tax and surtax as to incomes over the surtax exemption.
**Combining normal tax, surtax and victory tax as to incomes over exemption.

At the time that the holding period was reduced to six months, Congress did increase the maximum tax on long-term capital gains

182

from 15 percent to 25 percent—a mere pittance when compared with the confiscatory rates applicable to any appreciable quantity of earned income.

As has been noted before, the action of Congress in shortening the capital gain holding period merely set the stage for a later development. Hence, it was not until funds were available for speculation (when President Kennedy provided the "tax cut") that the speculation in common stocks hit the boiling point. It matters not whether the purchaser of stocks wanted low-taxed capital gains or an inflation hedge; either reason for purchasing stocks had to contribute toward creating an artificial demand.

The artificially reduced supply of inflation hedges also was caused by the Federal income tax. As previously mentioned, dividends paid on shares of stock are not a tax deduction to the paying corporation, whereas interest paid on corporate debt is tax deductible. This means that if a corporation borrows instead of selling additional shares of stock to raise capital, the cost of the capital (the interest) can be deducted as expense, and a large part thereof will be recovered by the corporation through a reduction in its income tax. There is not the same tax result for the cost of capital paid in the form of dividends. Accordingly, the income tax discouraged the practice of corporations selling shares to raise capital, and encouraged the raising of capital through borrowing. One can say, too, that the fewer the shares a corporation sells, the greater the "equity" for each share and the larger the potential capital gain appreciation.

Hence, corporations borrowed, and sold very few shares to raise cash for capital purposes. One of the largest corporate giants did not augment its corporate treasury by a single dime through the sale of additional common shares during the long period from the close of 1929 to the close of 1965. However, the value of the common shares of this corporate giant increased from about $4 billion at their 1929 high to $32.4 billion at their 1965 high. Of course, the shareholders of this corporate giant have benefited from the kiting of the market value of its shares, but the corporation itself has received no part of this increase in value.

In the case of another large corporation, the value of its shares

183

increased from about $220 million at their 1929 high to about $424 million at their 1965 high. During this long period, the second corporation sold additional shares to raise capital only to the extent of some $11.2 million. Certainly there is very little connection between an increase of share value of more than $200 million and the corporation's cash sale of shares for its capital needs to an extent of little more than $11 million. The condition of an artificially inspired demand for common stock vs. the artificially reduced supply of additional common shares for purchase can be rather convincingly demonstrated with statistics. All we need do is compare the dollar share-volume on the New York Stock Exchange with the amount of new capital raised by corporations through selling common shares during the same period, according to the Securities and Exchange Commission's published statistics. Here is such comparison:

TABLE 68

SHARE TRADING ON NEW YORK STOCK EXCHANGE
vs.
NEW CAPITAL OFFERINGS

Period Covered	Billions of Dollars of Shares Traded N.Y.S.E.*	New Corporate Capital Offerings During Period Covered**		
		Bonds	Preferred Stock	Common Stock
1942 year end to 1949 year end	74.6	29.30	4.06	3.64
1949 year end to 1965 year end	582.8	136.93	8.88	27.81
1965 year end to 1968 year end	368.9	54.76	2.10	7.83
Entire period of 1942 year end to 1968 year end	1,026.3	220.99	15.04	39.28

Sources: *From New York Stock Exchange publications.
　　　　**Securities and Exchange Commission data.

Imagine competing in a market for the purchase of common stocks to be used as inflation hedges under the condition that total dollar transactions over a period of time exceeded one trillion dollars,

184

whereas the new supply of common shares had increased by only $39 billion, or less than 4 percent of the total N.Y.S.E. dollar transactions. The conclusion is obvious that the mania for common stocks as inflation hedges and/or a source for low-taxed capital gains had caused the same shares to be traded over and over again (like used merchandise), but always at higher prices. Of course, during this period many corporations "went public" for the first time, which increased the shares available for purchase by the public; but someone had held these shares before the corporation "went public."

Having demonstrated how the market for common stocks was "rigged" by the income tax's creating an artificial demand for shares while simultaneously, and equally artificially, holding down the supply, I turn to the third risk of common-stock purchasers—that a large number of them had the purchasing power of a monopolistic organization.

I shall start that explanation by commenting that organizations with what I call monopolistic purchasing power are another economic aberration brought about by the Federal income tax. Such organizations are trusts and other funds holding securities purchased with tax-deductible dollars contributed by employers; the funds are intended to supply pensions for employees. Not only were the underlying monies tax deductible when contributed by the employer but, at that time, they also escaped tax as a form of deferred income to the employee beneficiaries of the funds. Finally, neither the interest nor dividend income of these employee funds, nor their capital gains, are subject to any income tax.

The taxpaying purchaser of common stocks must pay tax on his income before he has funds to invest, and his income and gains from investments must be sufficiently large to pay another income tax and leave something remaining as "net profit." This obviously places the taxpayer-investor at a competitive disadvantage with the tax-free employee trust funds in the struggle to get common stocks as inflation hedges.

However, those who bought common stocks as inflation hedges were paying no attention to these obstacles. Nor did they observe the fact that common-stock price increases bore little relationship to

185

budgetary inflation, i.e., the increase in the Consumer Price Index. This lack of relationship is revealed in the following tabulation:

TABLE 69

STOCK PRICE INCREASES vs. CONSUMER PRICE INCREASES

Period Covered	Increase in Consumer Price Index	Points Advanced in Consumer Price Index	Increase in Dow Jones Industrial Stock Price Index	Points Advanced Dow Jones Industrial Stock Index
1942 to 1949	56.8 to 83.0	26.2	119.71 to 200.52	80.81
1949 to 1965	83.0 to 109.9	26.9	200.52 to 969.26	768.74
1965 to 1968	109.9 to 121.9	12.0	969.26 to 985.21	15.95

This tabulation adds to the accumulation of evidence that after the year 1949 (which, from facts previously presented, was about the time that conservative business and financial procedures were discarded) the soaring stock market really got going. However, one could also note that the tight-money condition (after 1965) placed a brake against further stock-price increases.

It is interesting to note that during the period 1966 to 1968, when Dow Jones Industrials found the upward course difficult, the proportion of dollar volume of share transactions to the value of listed shares had appreciated considerably. This is shown in Table 70.

This data reveals how a massive share-trading volume had been built up over a period of years, with share trading showing an increase for almost every year in an eleven-year period. The share trading then literally exploded from 1966 to 1968 inclusive, causing a still higher turnover of the shares listed. The demand for shares represented by this huge trading volume should have propelled the prices of stocks upward, including those in the Dow Jones Industrial Average. This is precisely what happened. Rather, it did happen until the years 1966 to 1968 inclusive when, despite the highest share trading in history, the Dow Jones Industrial Index barely moved ahead.

Applying simple economics, as reflected in the law of supply and demand, the huge trading volume and share turnover during 1966

186

TABLE 70

NEW YORK STOCK EXCHANGE
DOLLAR VOLUME TURNOVER

Year	Year-End Market Value of Shares Listed	Market Value of Total Stock Traded During the Year, Including Odd Lots	Proportion of Value of Stock Traded During Year to Year-End Market Value
		(in billions of dollars)	
1958	276,665	32.754	11.8%
1959	307.708	43.476	14.1%
1960	306.967	37.960	12.4%
1961	387.841	52.699	13.6%
1962	345.846	47.341	13.7%
1963	411.318	54.887	13.3%
1964	474.322	60.424	12.7%
1965	537.481	73.200	13.6%
1966	482.541	98.565	20.4%
1967	605.817	125.329	18.1%
1968	692.337	144.978	20.9%

Source: Computed from New York Stock Exchange published data.

to 1968 represented an obvious demand for common stocks. However, the fact that share trades did take place in substantial volume, but with share prices practically stalemated, revealed, too, that the demand for shares was being counterbalanced by a supply of shares, otherwise share prices would have rocketed upward under the pressure of heavy buying volume. The almost stalemated condition of share prices simply revealed that quite a number of persons holding shares had become just as eager to sell as those wanting to buy shares were willing to purchase.

This should have been interpreted as a condition in which quite a number of persons believed that common-share prices had reached excessive levels. The expression of that belief prompted me to check with the New York Stock Exchange census that estimates the number of persons holding shares. According to the Stock Exchange census, the estimated number of shareholders increased from 20.12 million to 26.4 million during those same three years when share-trading volume hit fantastic levels and when the Dow Jones Indus-

187

trial Index was treading water for all practical purposes. Later (in 1970) the New York Stock Exchange census of shareholders estimated that as many as 30.8 million persons were shareholders.

It would appear somewhat absurd to conclude that the 6.28 million persons that had joined the ranks of common-stock shareholders during the years 1966 to 1968 were as informed and experienced on matters concerning common-stock purchases as were the older hands in the business of stock speculation. Rather, one should assume that these might be the typical "lambs" who had been attracted to stock purchasing as an easy road to riches. And they served the typical function of "lambs" in that they apparently bought the shares that long-time shareholders with considerably more experience were willing to sell. After the close of 1968, some additional millions of persons became shareholders for the first time.

All that has been said in this and in preceding chapters is borne out by an analysis of New York Stock Exchange data for the long period of 1942 to 1968. If this data is divided into different periods, we can note how the stock market reflected the increases in nonproductive spending by the government as well as the intent to acquire insurance against inflation via the inflation-hedge route. This is shown in Table 71.

There should be little question but what the drive to acquire inflation hedges (and/or low-taxed capital gains) contributed to the inflation of the economy. All speculation tends to affect the prices of everything, including consumer items. For example, the upward movements in the values of apartment houses and other rental real estate (other inflation hedges) must, of necessity, have increased rentals as each successive purchaser of a project paid a higher price and had to charge a higher rental in order to receive a reasonable income return on his investment. Somewhat similarly, the upward movement of common-stock prices places a burden upon the management of any corporation whose shares have increased in value. Obviously, these managements have to increase the income of the corporation to seek to justify the increased selling price of the corporation's common shares. And although this might not directly cause prices of the corporation's products to increase, one should respect

188

TABLE 71

RELATIONSHIP OF N.Y.S.E. SHARE TRADING TO DOW JONES INDUSTRIAL AVERAGE

Period Covered	Period in Terms of Years	N.Y.S.E. Billions of Dollars of Shares Traded During — Entire Period Covered	Average Per Year	Dollar Upward Progress (Increase) Dow Jones Industrial Average During Period Covered	Dollar Increase in Dow Jones Industrial Average Per Billion Dollars of Shares Traded
I. While conservative practices continued 1942 year end to 1949 year end	7	74.6	10.6	80.81	$1.08
II. The discard of conservatism 1949 year end to— 1955 year end	6	122.7	20.4	287.88	2.35
III. The economy begins to falter 1955 year end to 1959 year end	4	133.6	33.4	190.96	1.43
IV. The economy experiences more difficulty 1959 year end to 1963 year end	4	192.9	48.2	87.85	0.46
V. The Kennedy infusion of more inflation 1963 year end to 1965 year end	2	133.6	66.8	202.05	1.51
VI. The boom-bust pattern 1965 year end to 1968 year end	3	368.9	122.9	15.95	0.04

Source: Computed from New York Stock Exchange published data.

the fact that an increase in prices is a relatively simple way to increase any corporation's income and thereby to justify a higher selling price for the corporation's shares.

There is a statistical approach for demonstrating the relationship between speculation and the general economy. This approach does not indicate precisely when speculation has been overindulged, but it provides at least a hint in that direction. The procedure consists of taking certain definite times when stock prices hit a high level, as reflected by the Dow Jones Industrial Average, and then computing the relationship of the market value of shares listed on the New York

Stock Exchange with the annual G.N.P. at these specific times. Although I have, in this text, shown little respect for the reliability of G.N.P. from the standpoint of measuring true productivity, G.N.P. can, nevertheless, be employed for purposes of comparing national spending with the total value of all shares listed on the New York Stock Exchange.

For the comparison, I have chosen the following dates for the reasons stated:

Date	Reason
August 1929	Pre-Depression high for the Dow Jones Industrial Average
June 1932	Depression low, Dow Jones Industrial Average
March 1937	Depression period high for the Dow Jones Industrial Average (immediately before President Roosevelt attacked prices)
December 1954	Duplication of 1929 high for the Dow Jones Industrial Average
December 1968	All-time recent high for Dow Jones Industrial Average

How the market value of the listed shares on the New York Stock Exchange at the times specified above compared with the then level of Gross National Product or national spending is shown in Table 72.

It should be remembered that almost immediately after the value of the N.Y.S.E.-listed shares represented 87.0 percent of G.N.P. in August 1929, the 1929 stock market crash occurred. And when the listed shares had a value equal to 69.2 percent of G.N.P. in March 1937, a drop in prices followed.* However, when the 1929 Dow Jones highs were duplicated in late 1954, the market value of N.Y.S.E.-listed shares was only 46.5 percent of G.N.P. and no drop in prices resulted. Finally, at the time that the Dow Jones Industrials

---

*The serious collapse in stock prices really occurred immediately after Labor Day 1937, when the Dow Jones Industrial Average experienced one of the most serious percentage declines in stock market history.

TABLE 72

RELATIONSHIP OF MARKET VALUE OF N.Y.S.E.-
LISTED SHARES TO GROSS NATIONAL PRODUCT

Month and Year	Dow Jones Industrial Stock Average*	Total Market Value of Shares Listed on the New York Stock Exchange** (billions of dollars)	Annual Gross National Product*** (billions of dollars)	Proportion of N.Y.S.E. Value of Shares Listed to G.N.P.****
August 1929	381.17	89.668	103.1	87.0%
June 1932	41.22	15.633	58.0	27.0%
March 1937	194.40	62.468	90.4	69.2%
December 1954	404.39	169.149	364.8	46.5%
December 1968	985.21	692.337	865.7	80.0%

Sources: *Barron's Weekly.
    **New York Stock Exchange publications.
   ***Bureau of the Census.
  ****Author's computation.

reached their all-time high in December 1968, the market value of listed shares on the N.Y.S.E. represented another high percentage when related to G.N.P., that percentage being 80 percent (and just below the 87 percent established for August 1929), and thereafter stock prices tumbled.

Sometime after 1968, facts were disclosed that demonstrated how the artificial income-tax-inspired scarcity in shares available for purchase was coming to an abrupt end. These facts revealed that insiders were selling shares (through secondary offerings), and that corporations themselves had returned, at long last, to the conventional means of satisfying their capital needs through the sale of shares for cash, instead of through a further increase in borrowings.

For example, the issue of *Barron's* for October 4, 1971, stated that, on the basis of figures released by the Salomon Brothers investment firm, the secondary share offerings by "insiders" totaled a staggering $1.7 billion in the first half of 1971 compared with only $328 million in the first half of 1970. The same *Barron's*, in its October 18, 1971, issue, announced that new common-stock offerings for cash by corporations themselves totaled $8.2 billion for the twelve months ended with July 1971. This figure exceeded the total sales of shares by corporations for the entire three-year period of 1966 to 1968, inclusive.

Such a rather abrupt increase in the supply of common stocks should have caused a sharp break in stock prices. However, most persons holding common stocks were afraid to sell because of the threat of an even more rampant inflation. Hence, by that time (in 1971), the value of billions of dollars in common stocks, that had been kited by twenty-five years of nonproductive spending and the workings of the income tax, was being supported by the highly tenuous factor of fear—the fear that inflation would become even more severe.

Which brings us to consideration of how the holders of inflation hedges hope to come out whole in surviving inflation. The key to their problem is their ability to sell their hedges at the right time and at the right price. However, with many Americans having acquired many billions of dollars worth of inflation hedges purchased at high prices, just how can these billions of hedges be sold at the right time and at the right price?

The last question reminds me of an article published in the *Milwaukee Sentinel* of April 27, 1972, by Lloyd Larson, the Sports Editor. Mr. Larson commented about the multi-million-dollar prices reputedly paid for sports franchises that often operate at a loss or on a small amount of profit. In the article, Mr. Larson offered a possible suggestion for these high prices in the single sentence: "Or does he figure on getting enough from the next buyer to leave him with a comfortable profit via capital gains?"

Perhaps it is this same wishful thinking that has motivated the purchasers of common stocks; i.e., the shares purchased can always be resold at a higher price. Somehow this mania for inflation hedges reminds one of the dilemma that ultimately confronted the tulip speculators in Holland more than 300 years ago. As stated in the words of Charles Mackay:

> At last, however, the more prudent began to see that this folly could not last forever. Rich people no longer bought the flowers to keep

them in their gardens, but to sell them again at cent per cent profit. It was seen that somebody must lose fearfully in the end. As this conviction spread, prices fell, and never rose again. Confidence was destroyed, and a universal panic seized upon the dealers. . . .*

Somehow the Wall Streeters seem to have forgotten the realism reflected in their own catch phrase of some years back, to the effect that "the crowd is always wrong."

*From *Extraordinary Popular Delusions and the Madness of Crowds*, by Charles Mackay, published in 1841, and reprinted by L.C. Page and Company in 1932.

CHAPTER 12

What the American People Must Do to Stop the Complete Destruction of the Dollar

The contents of this book reveal the tragic story of how Americans have been deluded into believing that a continuous source of spending money could eliminate the need for people to undertake the normal efforts of working, producing and saving in order to provide this nation with a continuing prosperity. The cold statistical facts, as revealed in the preceding chapters, attest to the futility of this. The more that national spending has increased without the accompaniment of an actual increase in productivity that could satisfy consumer needs, the greater has been the drop in the value of the dollar. As a matter of fact, the decreasing value of the dollar has been directly brought about by nonproductive spending and nonproductive work activity, since these have increased costs and the higher costs have prompted prices to move ever higher.

The text should make clear, too, that the weakness in the value of the dollar, plus soaring prices, have really been announcing the deterioration in the total American economy, which, overwhelmed with debt, has been staggering from one crisis to another. This is the sorry record of "How the Government is Wrecking Your Dollar."

Nevertheless, many Americans who understand fully all about the havoc that government spending has wrought have done nothing except to complain to their friends about it. These same persons, however, will insist that there can be no future economic catastrophe because "the Government will spend itself out of every depression." As a matter of fact, these are the very persons who have acquired inflation hedges to provide them with insurance for economic survival.

The review of the American economy contained in this book should contribute in a small way to demolish the belief that government spending (as promoted by economic theorists) can go on indefinitely. The statistical facts presented herein clearly reveal a boom-bust economic pattern that is all set to bust. Further, that bust, whenever it may occur, is not going to be avoided by any more government spending *because the government has already spent funds in excess of the wealth available for spending.* Yes, the weakness in the dollar has been announcing to the world that the government's dollar-spending ammunition has become debilitated through overuse and abuse.

It is completely accurate to say that those in Government know that this spending cannot continue for long. This is revealed in the fact that those in Government have been tacitly admitting the pending bankruptcy of the Federal Government. The United States Government, like any debtor overwhelmed with financial obligations, has already begun to repudiate its promises and its obligations. For example, the government will not (and cannot) honor its promise to redeem foreign-held dollars with its insufficient gold supply. There are other examples—such as the Government has already refused to respect a law that would require it *permanently* to issue silver in exchange for its Silver Certificates; the Government has refused to acknowledge a legal obligation to maintain security behind the Federal Reserve notes; and the Government has substituted base metal for valuable metal in the American coinage system. Of course these repudiations were made legal, but how legal is it for a debtor to enact its own laws to renege on its promises. And no matter how glibly these recent actions by the Federal Government have been described to the American people, each of these actions demonstrated how those in the Federal Government were admitting a pending total insolvency of the government.

Of course, Americans hold private property worth billions of dollars. And, of course, that privately held property must be used to finance the government's continued spending. How else could a government whose spending exceeds its tax collections continue its spending, except by using privately held property to supplement a money that has lost its value? Yes, these remarks suggest that the government is apt to confiscate privately owned property to continue its spending. However, "confiscate" is an ugly word, so let us suggest instead that the Federal Government will buy the privately held property.* But this buying procedure would be something less than voluntary on the part of the seller. It would resemble the procedure whereby the government gave paper dollars to private citizens for their gold back in 1933. At that time the government paid about $20.50 per ounce for the gold, yet shortly thereafter officially proclaimed that gold was worth $35 per ounce.

Eventually all America, from the Federal Government to the lowliest citizen must become impoverished. This has happened before, to nations whose former greatness is now only reflected in the pages of history books, and this can happen to America.

But let us end this text on a note of optimism. The imminent threat of the government's seizure of privately held property can be avoided. Similarly, the American dollar can again be strengthened and occupy the position of respect it once held in the marts of the world. However, in order to accomplish such objectives, Americans must undertake to put an end to the experimentations of the economic theorists with the American economy and with American lives.

Considering first the identity of the economic theorists, the text makes clear that Federal Government officialdom has been directing

---

*Nevertheless, the public has already been prepared for confiscation without compensation, since it has been brainwashed into believing that property rights must yield to human rights. Of course, the public presumes that confiscation can affect only the rich —something like the income tax allegedly soaking only the rich.

the massive spending. Nevertheless, *the succession of U.S. Presidents have not thought up the multitude of spending theories.* Obviously, the theories had to be conceived by those who have been advising them. It is these theorists who, as consultants to the political leaders, have conceived the economic plans responsible for converting America from a highly productive world leader into a nation whose spending has far surpassed its productivity.

One need not search far to find an acknowledgment by a former political leader that economic theorists in government have been devising the economic game-plan. I refer to no less an authority than former President Lyndon B. Johnson who, in the course of a speech at Princeton University in 1966, rather proudly admitted:

> ... The 371 major appointments that I have made as President in the two-and-a-half years that I have occupied the office collectively hold 758 advanced degrees. . . . And so many are the consultants called from the ivy that a university friend of mine recently said to me, "At any given moment a third of the faculties of the United States are on a plane going somewhere to advise if not to consent."

In reading these words of former President Johnson, it needs to be stressed that his departure from the White House did not in the slightest change the process whereby government actions remain in the hands of the theorists; because the theorists who "call the economic plays" have never been elected by the people, they could not lose their status through a change of administrations. Without question, some theorists stopped advising the government after President Johnson's return to civilian life, but these were simply replaced by other theorists under a program that has been established for something like forty years. Even worse, as each theorist in turn has stopped advising the Federal Government, his reputation as a former adviser to the government has enabled him to pop up, sooner or later, as an adviser in social work, or even in industrial or financial enterprise, to continue undiminished his power and devotion to the cause of nonproductive spending.

If my words imply that national elections have become a futile exercise, because theorists will control the actions of the Federal

Government in any event, this is precisely what the words are intended to mean. Practically unnoticed is the fact that theorists, rather than officials elected to office, have controlled American economic actions for something like forty years. Yet, unless Americans can be convinced of that fact, they cannot ever hope to stop the impoverishment of their country that has virtually been completed by those theorists. Accordingly, at this point, the development of power by the theorists controlling the Federal Government shall be reviewed before I supply the only workable solution for Americans to save their dollar, their economy and their economic future.

The introduction of theorists into the Federal administration and the inception of government participation in economic procedures under the counsel of theorists on a grand scale started in 1933.* At that time, President Franklin Delano Roosevelt began the practice in a small way by delegating a group of "Brain Trusters" to help him solve the problems of the Great Depression. Admittedly, some of the original Roosevelt Brain Trusters had a practical slant on economic matters. However, the more practical theorists, in that first experiment of the Federal Government invading the competitive economic struggle, soon found themselves out of tune with the theorists who had no practical understanding, and the former departed from the Brain Trust. From that time to the present, all economic planning of the government has been under the control of persons endowed with theory only, and without the slightest attention having been paid by these theorists to the practical aspects of their planning.** Nor has it mattered much which political party has currently elected the Chief Executive of the United States.

It is quite paradoxical to acknowledge that theorists have, for some forty years, controlled all American economic actions, and simultaneously to insist that the very first application of pure theory to Ameri-

*There should be no question but that President Hoover, and even more so President Woodrow Wilson, had at least partially followed the views of theorists. Nevertheless, the occurrence of the Great Depression extended to the theorists a much broader power.
**Perhaps the best evidence of this is revealed in the pages of this text, and one can cite particularly the failure of President Kennedy's advisers to appreciate how the tax cut and the investment credit would cause a boom-bust economic development.

can economic affairs was a complete failure. It is true, nevertheless, that the small group of Brain Trusters who had continued to counsel President Roosevelt up until the start of World War II were still groping for a solution for the depression ills when the war started. By the start of World War II, the theorists had been unable appreciably to extricate America from the throes of the Great Depression. This was so, even though President Roosevelt had been careful to label the obvious resurgence of depression conditions in the latter part of the year 1937 as being a "recession."

Nevertheless, and as explained in a preceding chapter, the intervention of World War II and the prosperity that followed thereafter caused Americans to forget about the fumblings of the theorists during the Depression. This provided the unabashed theorists with the opportunity to claim that their advice had been responsible for postwar prosperity, and ever since then the theorists have taken credit for the continuous, but highly artificial, national prosperity. In the situation where the quality of that highly synthetic prosperity was never seriously questioned by the American public, the membership in the society of allegedly successful economic planners was allowed to expand greatly, and this acceptance of the theorists by the public impelled them to invade economic activity in many private sectors of the economy.

One should acknowledge, however, that the huge numerical expansion of American theoretical experts was considerably abetted through their being an offshoot of the great scientific, medical and engineering accomplishments that had marked the period of World War II and thereafter. Of course, it is easy to understand why their awesome scientific accomplishments had developed a great faith in, and respect for, the scientific experts in the physical sciences. However, less understandable is the reason why this faith and respect for scientists had been extended promiscuously, so as to rub off on the theorists serving as experts in all other areas of activity. Yet, every time that a scientific experiment has broadened human knowledge of the miracles of the universe, it has been assumed, too, that mere experimentation could uncover similar miracles in the areas of economics, sociology and other human relations. Whenever scientists in

199

the physical areas have found new ways to control natural and physical properties, it has been taken for granted that the economists and the sociologists could similarly undertake to control the actions of uncontrollable humans. Finally, since scientists with graduate degrees had helped uncover the miracles of the atomic world, it was imagined that graduate education could likewise uncover miracles in all other forms of activity, practically without limit.

In the midst of this weirdly expanding dedication to theory, there existed a notable incongruity. The experts in the physical sciences had to learn well the age-old rules developed for each particular science by prior generations of scientists, and it was these old, time-tested rules that the scientists have themselves tested, expanded, more precisely interpreted, reduced to more meaningful understanding, and then put to practical application. Contrariwise, the theoretical economists have, in fact, ignored the old rules established by their predecessors concerning the reaction of humans to economic and social conditions. For example, many of the present-day American economists have publicly stated that the "classical rules" of economics no longer apply.

Unfortunately for America, the great bulk of the American public has not resisted, but has in fact accepted this domination of their lives by experts. This can be more clearly demonstrated by taking a short detour from economics into the field of professional sports. There can be little question that in many well-publicized sports contests there are more experts involved, whether these be called commentators, sportswriters or some other name denoting expertise, *than there are sports contestants.* In a substantially similar manner to that in which the economic theorists have directed American economic affairs, these sports experts have told Americans how each game was won or why it was lost. This despite the fact that the innovation of the television screen was supposed to enable Americans to watch these contests directly and to decide on their own who won the game and why. Incidentally, this huge increase in the number of sports experts also has an economic facet, since the American consumer pays for all this sports expertise whether it is necessary or not and regardless if it is wanted. That conclusion is completely valid, because the principal support for the great number of American sports experts is in the compensation they receive from the advertisers of products, and the entire cost of the advertising is a part of the prices that the consumer pays.*

It is sad to note that this emphasis upon the experts in practically all walks of life has reduced Americans to an apathetic, impotent and bewildered lot without minds of their own. Americans, in following the lead of experts, have, for all practical purposes, shrugged off their own individual responsibilities. Yet some Americans wonder why their nation has been overrun with crime, loose moral conduct, pollution, major fires, death on the highways, and all of the other current national problems. Actually, these conditions are the telltale evidence of a people without personal responsibility. Quite pathetically, the nation's young have taken to marching and protesting about current conditions, but they are doing nothing more than demonstrating the very lack of personal responsibility that is the cause of their frustrations. Even worse, there has not been a solution offered for curing the national ills that does not require that still another expert, or body of experts, fortified with millions to spend, should undertake the task.

But let me return to the point of inquiry and more precisely indicate the source of power of the theorists who control American economic affairs. These consist of an elite of college graduates with multiple degrees who are members of a sort of supergovernment, and their power rests upon a firm foundation for quite a number of reasons.

Of utmost importance is the apparent unquestioned competence of these particular theorists. Since they are not engaged directly in any competitive struggle, whether in politics, business or otherwise, this means that they can neither be charged with failures nor credited with victories as could a politician, a businessman, a banker, a

---

*The advertising-conscious sports experts in the news media have their own way of belittling the value of the dollar. Hence, a reported "million dollar contract" makes an instant millionaire out of a sports figure, who, if he performs well, *might* earn $100,000 for each of ten years. Similarly, the news report that "Joe Blow Won the Hicksville $250,000 Open" must be carefully analyzed to learn that Joe Blow really received the $25,000 first prize.

professional man, a worker or a sports contestant. Hence, their apparent competence places their alleged expertise beyond question or criticism, and gives these noncompeting theorists an aura of respectable impartiality and godlike omniscience. Obviously, anyone may express a theory without fear of being condoned or chastised should the theory later prove to be inane or impractical, since any theory is nothing more than an untested, and generally unsupported, opinion. Moreover, the theories of those in the economic elite of government have a practically untouchable quality for still another reason, and that is that they generally hold multiple academic degrees as their badge of wisdom. Finally, the "proof of the pudding" of their opinions generally follows by a considerable number of years after the opinion was first offered or initially put into practice, so that there is discontinuity between the experiment with the opinion and whatever disaster or success that experiment ultimately yields. For example, the boom-bust American economic pattern has trailed by several years the introduction of the investment credit and the tax cut by President Kennedy's advisors.

Further, the theorists enjoy a monopoly in the court of public opinion. This is so because the public has been so propagandized that it criticizes or ignores the viewpoints of anyone engaged in a competitive struggle on the ground that what he says is biased, partial and dictated by a selfish interest. On the other hand, however, the public has been thoroughly indoctrinated to treat the views of theorists with the utmost respect.* This obvious fact is manifested by the very people who have sought to overthrow the actions of the theorists, for even they have considered it necessary to employ another group of theorists to contest the theories expressed by the alleged "economic experts" in government.**

*This is a carryover from the humble objectivity formerly credited to college professors. However, that image ignores the fact that those who practice pure theory now enjoy emoluments and rewards second to none. They enjoy worldwide recognition and publicity; they are honored guests in the drawing rooms of social and national leaders, and even the White House; they travel extensively and without costs; and their continued livelihood, if not actual wealth, has become permanently endowed.
**So-called "right wing" Americans have spent millions of dollars in an attempt to warn other Americans against the actions of liberally inclined theorists. However, even these millions had to be contributed to nonproductive activity, since one group of theorists was paid to oppose a different breed of theorists.

President Johnson acknowledged this monopoly of the theorists when he spoke about the testimony they offered. That testimony has controlled practically every law enacted by Congress. Oftentimes some theorists have testified for, and others against, a particular bill in Congress so as to give added strength to the image of objectivity that has practically deified the viewpoints of the theorists. And while Americans have listened with rapt attention to the publicized debates of prominent theorists, sometimes expressing opposing economic solutions, *the practical answers to many economic problems have been denied publicity, so that the practical solutions never came into the open.*

Of course, since the economic theorists in government were well fortified with academic degrees (again as President Johnson acknowledged), these theorists have automatically obtained the unlimited and unqualified backing of those in the academic world. Nor need it be doubted that the apparent impartiality of the theorists found wide acceptance by the clergy. Perhaps of the greatest importance in disseminating the views of the theorists among the public at large was the readiness with which the news media would repeat and broadcast far and wide every thought expressed by any well-known theorist. Again, this reflected an "image of impartiality," supplemented by an alleged expertise resting principally upon a college degree. Meanwhile, there can be no question but that the productive sector of the American economy has been bearing the cost (through paying for the advertising) of disseminating the very news and philosophies that are contributing to the annihilation of the American productive system.

This text has already emphasized the abnormal expansion of American institutions of higher learning. Since theorists have been placed on a pedestal of sort, the number of persons seeking college degrees, and particularly graduate degrees, has expanded without limit, and Ph.D. degrees have proliferated to cover every theoretical (and generally nonproductive) activity possible. Americans have deified education without demanding a scintilla of proof that a mass production of college graduates could contribute in any meaningful respect toward American productivity and well-being. Everyone needed a college degree (and preferably a doctor's degree*) no matter what the cost to the nation in terms of direct expense, and the horrendous indirect cost of this abnormal extension of nonproductivity.**

Most important of all, however, has been the theorists' influence upon the Federal Government, as it was the subject of comment by President Johnson. In their role as government advisers, the theorists have posed as unbiased, impartial experts and they have continuously advocated a massive spending of money by the government. Hence, they were tailor-made to advance the continued election of any politician to office, because spending brings votes and votes are needed to win an election. How much better for a politician to request that the government spend in accordance with a spending plan advocated by an allegedly unbiased theorist *than for the politician to admit that the spending was necessary for the completely selfish purpose of getting himself reelected to office!*

Certainly—the economic theorists are right in concluding that spending is needed to keep an economy moving, but one does not need to be a graduate-degree economist to know that. However, something more than spending is required to keep the American economy strong and healthy, and the most important thing also needed is a highly efficient productive machine that is manned by trained and experienced workmen, from the lowliest laborer to the top executives.***

The theorists have never acknowledged that a nation peopled by too many theorists could not supply a well-balanced economic ma-

*This absurd emphasis on doctorates is best demonstrated by the procedure of certain law schools in offering a Doctorate of Law degree upon payment of a small fee by Bachelor of Law graduates who left these law schools several decades earlier. The author refused to accept this retroactive labeling of his academic accomplishments.
**Repeating what was said in an earlier chapter, *The Morgan Guaranty Survey* for June 1971 stated that the budgets for all institutions of higher learning increased from just over $4 billion in 1955 to $27 billion in 1971, and Federal funds to the higher schools swelled from $500 million in 1955 to $4.4 billion in 1968.
***The theorists' objective of "full employment" seems most desirable from a social aspect. Unfortunately, however, where workers are assured of full employment, they lack the incentive to develop their capabilities fully. The sports experts regularly acknowledge that a "hungry athlete" is the most apt to succeed. Somewhat similarly, minimum pay scales and uniform wage rates discourage top-grade performance. Even the Soviet Union has learned these truths.

chine. They have not admitted the importance to an economy of craftsmen and those in productive, as well as those in nonproductive, work activities. Nor have the theorists ever noticed that there must be a balance between the amounts expended for the cost of production of the goods and services needed and wanted by consumers as opposed to the "overhead costs" of an economy, the latter being reflected in the cost of operation of government and of other nonproductive enterprise, including nonprofit organizations.

Employing the cruel advantage of hindsight, one could readily contend that the theorists, for something like forty years, have been engaged in their original project of avoiding another depression, and in all that time they have not changed the direction of the objectives employed to reach that end. So we find that the original Brain Trusters decided, in 1933, that the American productive plant was overbuilt and that the economy needed only the revitalization of spending. And, ever since 1933, the theorists have ignored the importance of a productive plant and have encouraged, instead, a continuing nonproductive spending. Of course, in 1933 the theorists were right in discouraging tight-fisted saving by depression-frightened Americans, so as to revitalize the then-depressed economy with spending. However, after prosperity reappeared, the theorists should have appreciated the need for encouraging saving and discouraging spending because of the altogether different condition of the national prosperity.

Again, the theorists were right in recognizing that, in 1933, trained and experienced workmen were too numerous for the economy of that day to absorb, and incentives for good worker performance were not needed at that time. However, this was no reason for the theorists assuming ever since then that trained and experienced workmen would always be available and that incentives for good and conscientious worker performance would never be needed. Yes, in 1933 there were some truly poor people who needed help, but the return of an enormous prosperity since then should have discouraged using poverty as the principal target in the theorists' advocacy of massive nonproductive spending.

Illogical though it may seem to one inclined to be logical, this

205

process of doing the same thing for forty years on end has been described by the theorists and their political allies as being progressive and modern, and sometimes referred to as "an expansion of new frontiers."* In spite of these fine-sounding labels, however, the theorists' continued emphasis upon nonproductive spending has had the practical effect of "turning back the clock" for the American productive machine.

Once again, there is here a confrontation between the gratifying image of an American economy that has been modernized and the totally different *result* of an American productive enterprise stumbling along in archaic fashion. And this paradox is the result of the theorists' stressing increased consumption, but without acknowledging that it requires an updating and improving of the productive machine. Perhaps a simpler analogy would say that the theorists have been so busy distributing the golden eggs that the fabled goose (the American productive machine) has produced that they have failed to consider the need for feeding that goose (updating, improving and expanding American productivity).

There can be little doubt that the theorists' spending has resulted in an American economy that overemphasizes consumption.** This condition should be apparent in the abnormal expansion in shopping centers, supermarkets, advertising, drive-in food-dispensing units, franchise units of various types, motels, resorts, and other leisure-satisfying or sports-promoting activities. All of these ventures are, for the most part, parasitical in that they would be useless without the production of that part of the economy that turns out in more meaningful fashion the more basic goods and services needed for human survival. Many of the ventures that stress consumption have not been

---

*The economists have sometimes described their activity as "fine-tuning" the economy. However, one leading economist has acknowledged, "I believe that we economists in recent years have done vast harm—to society at large and to our profession in particular—by claiming more than we can deliver." Stated more simply, an elite of self-appointed intellectuals has been trying to play the part of God.
**This, more than anything, has thrown the support of those in retail trade and, more particularly, those in advertising behind the spending by the theorists. Meanwhile, this nation's industrialists have been literally lampooned by the news media whenever the industrialists have expressed a more conservative approach to spending. The industralists can get fair play only in trade publications that have limited circulation.

the result of years of development but are the outgrowth of some idea that, supplemented with dollars, has created a "business." Often the owners of these types of business serve no purpose other than to take the risk of loss, or to benefit from the profit, since the business judgment needed for their operation has been supplied in canned form from a central headquarters that dispenses the franchise at a price.

Meanwhile, however, the productive sector of the American economy has not experienced an expansion similar to that of the economic sector that distributes goods for consumption. In the productive sector, America is fast losing, if it has not already lost, its technological leadership in the world, and America is no longer able to compete with foreign producers, whether from the standpoint of quality or price, or both.* In the productive sector there has not occurred any vast expansion in number of businesses, but rather there has been a severe factor of contraction in that giant conglomerates now dominate the productive part of the American economy. As a matter of fact, many industrial corporations have branched out so as to share in the profits of the consumptive sector with the hope of their continued survival by so doing.

Of course, the theorists have an answer for this obvious overexpansion of consumptive enterprises and the underexpansion in productive activities. The theorists reason that the mass-production proclivities of American industry can furnish all the goods that are needed without any perceptible expansion. Not only is that the easy answer, but it also happens to be the only answer the theorists have had since 1933 when they first invaded the American economic world.

This easy answer of the theorists conveniently ignores the fact that the theorists themselves have contributed to the lack of development in the American productive sector. For example, the theorists have not acknowledged that American industry has been overwhelmed by the cost of nonproductivity and has been denied ade-

*That conclusion even applies to the drug industry where, according to an article entitled "Global Medicine Chest" (Barron's of July 31, 1972), the United States has slipped in the discovery and use of new drugs as compared with other nations, despite an increase in annual research expenditures of from $227 million in 1960 to $550 million in 1970.

207

quate capital and manpower because these have been diverted to nonproductive enterprise. Hence, American industry had to turn to the only course remaining—the overexpansion of mass production. It is this more than anything that has resulted in American goods having inferior quality, a stark sameness, that, when high priced too, could not possibly compete in international markets. Even worse, these products could not even compete in America, because the foreign imports had better quality, offered more selectivity, and had a lower price.*

Had American industry been able to use the dollars and the manpower diverted to nonproductive pursuits, industry could have undertaken sufficient research and development to retain its standing as a world technological leader. Instead, industry has tried to advance through an exploitation of development completed as early as during the Great Depression, yet later supplemented by World War II developments obtained through Federal Government funds for research, plus whatever limited research American industry has been able to finance on its own.

The plight of American industry, as described above, is proved by quite a number of demonstrable factors. For example, it is so costly, if not impossible, for industry to develop new business ventures that most corporations have acquired other businesses rather than undertaking to build an additional business. This, better than anything, explains the growth of "conglomerates." Analogous to the corporate shares that have been turned over and over by speculators at successively higher prices, entire corporate business ventures have, like used merchandise, been sold and resold, always at higher prices.**

And, being deprived of expansion opportunities at home, American industry has moved to foreign nations. One of these acts of desperation by American corporations involved the exportation of

*According to estimates for the year 1971, in that year the United States lost its world leadership in the machine-tool industry. The U. S. dropped from first place to third in machine-tool production, and from first place to fourth in machine-tool consumption.

**The Federal income tax has encouraged tax-free mergers and the sale of businesses for cash, with the profit taxed at low long-term capital gain rates, for any business owners overwhelmed by the difficulties of owning and operating a business.

jobs to workers in foreign nations.* However, in other instances, entire American plant operations have been moved to foreign soil as a last-ditch effort on the part of American corporations to survive.

Let it be repeated that it would be a completely idle hope for Americans to believe that they can ultimately eliminate the work of theorists in government by casting ballots at some future election. This has been demonstrated as futile at each election. There have been nine national elections since 1933, and the theorists are more firmly entrenched in control of the economy now than ever before. It needs to be repeated, too, that it is also idle thought to presume that Americans can continue to sidestep the ultimate fatality of national impoverishment that these economic procedures will bring.

The American economy must be revitalized to restore the American dollar to a money with value, and to remove the artificiality in the economy induced by the spending of the theorists. To accomplish this, the demand for goods and services must be equated with the supply. This means that the power to spend must be taken from the government and returned to the American public so that the people can again exercise the decision as to what types of goods and services are to be purchased. And the purchases by American consumers shall control the production needed to satisfy their purchases. It is required to restore to the workers, too, the discretion as to what part of their earnings are to be spent and what part saved. These various steps are necessary to enable the American public to control that portion of its earnings that is to be expended on the overhead expense of the economy, i.e., the cost of government and other instrumentalities of nonproductivity. Only in this way can the continued wreckage of the dollar, and the ultimate impoverishment of all Americans, be stopped.

Perhaps the foregoing requirements for removing the artificiality in the American economy could be considerably simplified by expressing the conclusion that *all Americans should have the freedom*

*According to news reports, an American manufacturer has received the consent of the U.S. Defense Department to have hardware for the Safeguard antimissile system made in Hong Kong because of the high American costs!

of spending or saving their earnings. * This freedom has been taken from them through the Federal income tax, which has transferred the decision to spend or to save to the Federal Government; but, actually, that decision has been exercised by the theorists advising the government. It is interesting to note that the late Franklin Delano Roosevelt, in his message to Congress on January 6, 1941, expressed the hope that a future world could be founded upon four essential freedoms: Freedom of speech and expression; freedom to worship God; freedom from want; and freedom from fear. But he failed to mention that important freedom to spend or save one's own money. Had Americans retained the freedom to spend or to save their own money, i.e., their earnings, the American economy could not have become overburdened with the artificiality of massive spending by the theorists.

It is entirely possible for Americans to rescue their economy from the depths in which it has become mired. Americans have done so before on several occasions. But for Americans to do that, the freedom to spend or to save must be restored to them to eliminate the stranglehold of the theorists upon the American economy.

There is only one way to accomplish the restoration to Americans of the freedom to spend or to save their earnings, and that is to abolish completely the Federal income tax upon the workers' incomes. Americans still have the freedom to demand this by requesting the legislative bodies of their own states to set in motion the elimination of the Sixteenth (income tax) Amendment to the United States Constitution. The elimination of that much-perverted Federal income tax is the only step that can restore to the workers control over their earnings and the power to spend their earnings for what they want; and to stop the spending for what some theorists shall decide that Americans should want. There is no other way to remove the artificial costs that are degrading the American economy to that of a third-class nation, and that will eventually destroy all American

---

*By propaganda, the theorists have thwarted the otherwise natural inclination of Americans to demand the freedom to keep or to spend the income earned by each person. That propaganda lampoons "property rights" and deifies "human rights," but without acknowledging that the right to own property *is* a human right.

property, the workers' incomes, and even affect American lives.

I will venture to say that there is hardly an American who truly understands the vicious manner in which the Federal income tax, resting solely upon the false image that it "soaks the rich," has impoverished American workers, has denied these workers the opportunity to save, and has even denied the workers the right to spend their earnings. And very few Americans know that the Federal income tax has completely warped and twisted all business and economic transactions. What greater proof can there be that the Federal income tax has not, in fact, soaked the rich than to refer to the fact that this tax has enabled wealth to become more concentrated than ever before.* Despite the crushing burden of the income tax upon large amounts of income *earned through actual work*, nevertheless the income tax has so permitted the amassing of fortunes that America has more millionaires than ever before.

After the Federal income tax has been abolished, the next step is for the American public to insist that any tax that is substituted for the income tax be restricted to the collection of revenues needed for Government operation only. This means that the new tax should not repeat the basic evil of the income tax and collect many billions in revenues beyond those needed for strictly governmental functions; that would directly encourage a spending by the Federal Government that is completely unrelated to the conduct of government. Unless the new tax is so restricted, government spending would continue but with the means for spending obtained through a different form of tax.

The public must insist, too, that the tax that is substituted for the income tax shall be formulated to collect taxes only. This means that, unlike the income tax, the new tax should not be subject to continuing changes that are designed to encourage or to discourage the free exercise by the public (and by those in business) of the freedom to save or the freedom to spend. Further, the new tax must be a direct tax so that the person paying it cannot pass on the tax he pays to the American consumer. This would make certain that at all times the

*Perhaps this is why many of the entrenched wealthy have supported the spending by the theorists.

taxpayers who are paying the new tax would know how much in taxes they are paying and that the taxes are coming out of their funds alone.

Finally, the new tax should be so designed as to be simple in its administration and with a low cost for collecting it, and the new tax should be difficult to avoid or to evade. These factors are essential to discard forever the multiple and complex regulations and the thousands of controversies and court contests that have been the hallmarks of the Federal income tax.

It would not be difficult to design a tax as described above. A sales or transactions tax would most readily meet the qualifications of such a new tax. A sales or transactions tax would be simple to administer, easy to interpret, have a low cost of collection, could not readily be avoided or evaded, and, most important of all, *that form of tax would leave no doubt in the public mind as to how much the tax is and who is bearing its burden.*

Also acceptable, although susceptible of being passed on to the consumer, is a gross income tax. However, to avoid the passing-on-to-the-consumer evil and some of the other difficulties experienced with the income tax, the gross income tax should be levied upon gross income *without any deductions and at a low rate.* Otherwise, a gross income tax would be nothing more than a form of improvement upon the present Federal income tax. As a matter of fact, the type of gross income tax above described is really the prototype that the framers of the Sixteenth (income tax) Amendment had in mind when the Federal income tax was first enacted for ratification by the several states.

The elimination of the Federal income tax and the substitution of another form of tax would immediately extricate from the American price structure the income taxes that have become imbedded therein. There can be no question that such a development would cause an economic upheaval—call it a serious economic depression if you will. That conclusion means that the elimination of the Federal income tax would automatically require a new price structure for all goods and services from whose price structure the Federal income tax has been removed. A rough guess would be that all prices would decline in the neighborhood of 30 percent or more. Of course, the consumer would benefit from these lower prices, but part of the benefit would be absorbed by the new tax. Nevertheless, the amount of that new tax would be far less than the dollars removed from the price structure through termination of the income tax.

Unless the tax structure is changed, however, Americans must accept an already admitted bankruptcy of the Federal Government and the eventual total impoverishment of the body public. The latter condition spells economic death for America, a condition far more serious than the economic unpleasantness, such as a depression, that will accompany the legal surgery to the tax structure that will enable America to survive. Certainly another depression is far less serious than the economic death that spells total impoverishment of the nation.*

Whether Americans choose to apply surgery to the tax structure, and knowingly experience the difficulties of economic readjustment, or prefer instead that the remaining wealth continue to be wasted away, whatever happens must be charged to the account of the theorists in government who have placed the American economy in its present predicament. Should the theorists want to deny that they are responsible for the economic ills that are already prevalent, it is appropriate to repeat the prophetic words previously quoted, as these were offered by the then U. S. Budget Director, Lewis Douglas, more than thirty-five years ago:

> The Government, by its fiscal policies, has deliberately laid the base for another inflation on a scale so gigantic that the bubble of the 1920s may finally seem small by comparison. We are now evidently going to have bigger and more painful inflation under Government sponsorship and induced by direct Government action. The New Deal is only the former "New Era" dressed up in different clothes. When the next bubble bursts, let it not be forgotten that the responsibility lies directly at the door of the present Administration.

*The twenty-five-year public image of continuous prosperity is completely false. Actually, a fictional prosperity has resulted from the government dissipating national wealth in spending to avoid depressions. If continued, this process will eventually cause national wealth to cease to exist.

Although many years have elapsed since the quoted words were publicly expressed, the facts about the economy summarized in this text should suggest that the time "when the next bubble bursts" is now. Yes, the economic bubble has already started to burst and the process will continue no matter what Americans may do. However, Americans have it within their power to prevent such bursting of the economy as will totally destroy American economic survival by eliminating the Federal income tax. Only through that action can Americans avoid a total national impoverishment and retain the chance to reorganize American economic affairs. Finally, if Americans should continue to tolerate the spending by theorists in government of the income tax dollars taken from workers, and allow these theorists to undertake some additional perversions of the American productive machine, there will not be much remaining in America to reorganize.

Of course, in either circumstance Americans will continue to live. But if the choice of Americans should be to continue the income tax and suffer the privations that continued economic theorism must bring, the suggestion that Americans would merely "exist" would be more appropriate. This is so because living under the chaos that would accompany national poverty would of necessity lead to a new form of American government. Perhaps that new form of government can be best described by my quoting some words spoken by Herbert Hoover during a discussion between Hoover and me that took place some years ago. This is how Hoover described a possible change in government:

> Unless the American people wake up mighty quickly they are ready for the man on horseback, and let us hope that it is a somewhat kindly fellow like DeGaulle rather than a madman like Hitler.

It is more appropriate to end this woeful tale about the wreckage of your dollar by expressing the hope that Americans will not allow a government by dictatorship to be forced upon them. However, with that hope must be included a prayer to the Almighty that Americans shall, by legal means, terminate the existence of the Federal income tax and establish a new "Magna Carta" that, like its English predecessor, shall remove the American people from a tyranny: the tyranny of a tax system that has denied Americans the right to their earnings.

Index of Tables

221

Table   Subject